The Complete
UK Air Fryer Cookbook
for Beginners

Flavourful & Simple Air Fryer Recipes for Every Meal | Vegetarian, Snacks, Sweet Treats, Holiday & Party and Family Favourites

(Full Colour Edition)

Lilly Gray

Copyright © 2024 By Lilly Gray
All rights reserved.

No part of this book may be reproduced, transmitted,
or distributed in any form or by any means
without permission in writing from
the publisher except in the case of brief quotations embodied
in critical articles or reviews.

Legal & Disclaimer

The content and information in this book is
consistent and truthful,
and it has been provided for informational,
educational and business purposes only.

The illustrations in the book are from the
website shutterstock.com,
depositphoto.com and freepik.
com and have been authorized.

The content and information contained
in this book has been compiled from reliable sources,
which are accurate based on the knowledge,
belief, expertise and information of the Author.
The author cannot be held liable
for any omissions and/or errors.

TABLE OF CONTENT

Introduction 1

Chapter 1: The Air Fryer Basics 3
What Is an Air Fryer? 3
How to Use an Air Fryer? 4
Why Do You Need an Air Fryer? 3
Even Cooking in an Air Fryer 6
How Do They Work? 4
How to Clean an Air Fryer? 7

Chapter 2: Breakfast Dishes 8
Classic Yorkshire Puddings 8
Grilled Herb Mushrooms on Toast 12
British Breakfast Frittata 8
Crispy Cheese and Bacon Scones 12
Sizzling Bacon and Egg Muffins 9
Savoury Baked Beans on Cheesy Toast 13
Crispy Black Pudding Bites 9
Baked Spinach and Feta Omelette 13
Luxurious Baked Avocado Eggs 10
Sumptuous Sausage and Egg Casserole 14
Crispy Grilled Bacon Sandwiches 10
Grilled Cheese and Tomato Breakfast
Sausage and Bean Breakfast Casserole 11
   Sandwiches 14
Full English Breakfast Traybake 11

Chapter 3: Lunch Dishes 15
Modern Ploughman's Lunch 15
Smoky Kippers and Eggs 18
Courgette and Ricotta Melts 15
Asparagus and Parma Ham Spirals 19
Herb-Crusted Air-Fried Fish 16
Orchard Pork Sausages with Rustic Mash .. 19
Lemon Zest Herb Chicken 16
Pub-Style Beef and Ale Hand Pies 20
Deluxe Ham and Cheese Toastie 17
Luxurious Welsh Rarebit Toasts 20
Crispy Veggie Galette 17
Minty Air Fried Lamb Chops 21
Quick Shepherd's Pie 18
Cheesy Onion Pie 21

Chapter 4: Dinner Dishes 22
Grilled Gammon with Garden Peas and
   Rosemary Jus 25
   Silky Hollandaise 22
Parsnip and White Wine Guinea Fowl 25
Ale-Braised Beef Brisket 22
Whisky Glazed Short Ribs 26
Duck with Orange Sauce 23
Lemon-Thyme Roasted Chicken 26
Thai Coconut Chilli Chicken 23
Dill and Lemon Infused Salmon 27
Barbecue Pork Belly 24
Colourful Stuffed Pepper Medley 27
Herb-Crusted Sea Bream 24
Satay Roast Chicken 28
Lamb Shoulder Feast with Peppered
Orchard Roast Pork with Cider Apples 28

Chapter 5: Vegan and Vegetarian Dishes 29
Toasted Sourdough and Hazelnut Asparagus
Golden Honey-Tahini Cauliflower 30
   29
Spiced Aloo Tikki Bites 31
Marmite and Poppy Seed Parsnips 29
Healthy Wholemeal Loaf 31
Pear and Chestnut Festive Stuffing 30
Balsamic Glazed Tofu and Gnocchi 32

Satay-Style Whole Cauliflower 32
Veggie Moussaka 33
Beetroot and Lentil Veggie Burgers 33
Savoury Nut Carrot Bites 34
Cider-Braised Veggie Sausage Hotpot 34
Herbed Polenta and Mushroom Bake 35
Summer Vegetable Gratin 35

Chapter 6: Snacks and Starters 36

Feta and Honey Filo Parcels 36
Golden Air-Fried Scotch Eggs 36
Creamy Boursin-Stuffed Mushrooms 37
Smoky Chilli Chips with Garlic Dip 37
Crispy Pakora Bites 38
Five-Spice Whitebait 38
Cheese and Cranberry Fondue Star 39
Spicy Nut and Seed Mix 39
Smoked Salmon Crostini 40
Bengali Beetroot Croquettes 40
Camembert Bread Bowl 41
Spiced Cauliflower Fritters 41
Paneer and Pepper Skewers with
   Gooseberry Raita 42
Chaat Platter 42

Chapter 7: Desserts and Sweet Treats 43

Lemon Meringue Tartlets 43
Rhubarb and Custard Brioche Bake 43
Blueberry Bliss Cheesecake 44
Pear and Butter Puff Strudel 44
Apple Hazelnut Galette 45
Black Forest Bakewell Delight 45
Caramelised White Chocolate Dream Cake ... 46
Japanese Fluffy Cheesecake 46
Honeyed Flapjacks 47
Zesty Lemon Drizzle Cake 47
Blackberry Millefeuille Delight 48
Honeyed Figs with Sesame Crunch 48
Classic Lemon Tart 49
Apple Crumble Cupcakes 49

Chapter 8: Holiday and Party Dishes 50

Chocolate Yule Log 50
Bacon-Wrapped Roast Turkey 50
Hasselback Swede Gratin 51
Cheese Mustard Straws 51
Turkey Koftas with Cranberry Dip 52
Cheesy Salmon Wreath 52
Game Terrine with Brandy Prunes 53
Creamy Bacon Sprouts 53
Walnut Cheese Rolls 54
Halloumi Clementine Salad 54
Crab Croquettes with Romesco Sauce 55
Lemon Sage Potatoes Anna 55
Festive Fruit Cake 56
Creamy Baked Leeks 56

Chapter 9: Family Favourites 57

Chicken and Mushroom Mini Pies 57
Favourite Sausage Roll Wreath 57
Peppered Steak and Radish Salad 58
Smoked Mackerel Melts 58
Eton Mess Roll 59
Lemon Curd Cake 59
Garlic Butter Chicken Kiev 60
Homemade English Muffins 60
Savoury Sausage Rolls 61
Rosemary and Sea Salt Flatbread 61
Herb-Crusted Roast Beef 62
Lemon Herb Roast Chicken 62
Banana Hot Cross Bread 63
Salmon Terrine Delight 63

Appendix 1: Measurement Conversion Chart 64

Appendix 2: Air Fryer Cooking Chart 65

Appendix 3: Recipes Index 67

Introduction

I am delighted to present this cookbook, specially curated for the UK audience. The Complete UK Air Fryer Cookbook for Beginners was born out of my passion for cooking and my unwavering belief in the power of the air fryer. Over the years, I have witnessed firsthand the transformative impact this remarkable appliance has had on my cooking and the meals I serve to my loved ones. Now, I am thrilled to share my knowledge, experiences, and a multitude of recipes with you all.

As an experienced chef, I have had the privilege of working in various professional kitchens, honing my skills and exploring different cooking techniques. However, it was the air fryer that truly captured my imagination and pushed the boundaries of my culinary creativity. Its ability to produce irresistibly crispy and golden textures, while minimising the need for excessive oil, has been nothing short of revolutionary.

In this cookbook, you will find an array of recipes that showcase the versatility and ingenuity of the air fryer. From classic comfort foods to exotic culinary delights, each recipe has been carefully crafted and tested to ensure delicious results that will leave you craving more. Moreover, this cookbook goes beyond just providing recipes; it is a comprehensive guide that equips you with the knowledge and techniques to get the most out of your air fryer.

So, my dear friends, I urge you to embark on this culinary adventure with me. Let this cookbook be your gateway to a world of culinary innovation, where you can indulge your creativity, experiment with new ingredients, and discover exciting flavours. Whether you are seeking quick weeknight meals, impressive dinner party delights, or delightful treats for your loved ones, this cookbook has you covered.

Chapter 1: The Air Fryer Basics

What Is an Air Fryer?

An air fryer is a worktop convection oven that comes in different sizes. Without the excess grease and oil that comes with deep-frying, it is intended to mimic the technique. The air fryer's fan circulates hot air quickly, giving food an outside coating that is crisp. Food is cooked rapidly and uniformly with air fryers because of the concentrated heat source. Here are a few examples of what you can create:

- Baked foods such as doughnuts, biscuits, and cakes
- Meats like steak, chicken wings, and pork chops
- Sides like potatoes and garlic bread

Of course, you can cook much more than that. For more to find, you will have to check my exclusive air fryer recipes from this cookbook.

Why Do You Need an Air Fryer?

The popularity of air fryers is at its prime! All around the world, more and more people are bringing air fryer home to cook healthy, crispy and oil-free meals. These little cooking appliances have revolutionised cooking technology, and now you can find the air-frying option in almost every other cooking appliance you purchase. All of this is happening due to the following most amazing benefits of air fryers:

- **Healthier**

An air fryer uses significantly less oil than a deep fryer, which is its principal health advantage. A large portion of the used oil also drains away without being absorbed by the food. As a result, you consume fewer calories and fat. These fryers' convection method encourages the Maillard reaction, a chemical process that results in browning. This has the added benefit of making the food look better while also enhancing its flavour while having less fat.

- **More Crispy Food**

Being able to generate crispy food without using oil is one of the best features of air fryers. They accomplish this by enclosing food in a perforated basket or on a rack with extremely hot air from all sides, using convection-style heating. As a result, air fryers are ideal for producing crispy chips, onion rings, fish fingers, and other conventional fried food kinds. Because it can cover the entire surface of the meal and because the frying basket allows any excess fat to drop away, an air fryer yields crispier results than a conventional convection oven.

- **Quicker**

Air fryers cook food far more quickly than the majority of traditional alternative ways because of how they operate. The rapid frying procedure is made possible by maintaining and constantly circulating the tremendous heat generated inside the fryer. Many versions either don't need to be heated up before use or only take a little time to do so. Compared to a conventional oven, cooking times can be reduced by more than 30 to 50 per cent, depending on the particular meal.

- **Clutter-free**

Compared to deep fryers, air fryers are much less dirty. That is because the cooking procedure only requires a small amount of oil, and it's this that makes the bulk of the mess. An air fryer may be cleaned most easily with a soft-bristle brush, dish soap, and water.

- **Safer**

Air fryers are generally safer because they are self-contained appliances and because little hot fat is used in the cooking process. Splashes and burns are less of a problem. In order to prevent the food from burning, machines are also made to turn off when the timer expires.

- **More Flexible**

An air fryer can be used to prepare most dishes that are typically cooked in a deep fryer just as well or even better. There are numerous recipes to experiment with. Surprisingly, baked items, vegetables, and steaks all performed nicely.

- **Retain Heat and Odour**

Air fryers retain heat, so unlike conventional ovens, they don't raise the temperature of your kitchen. If you reside in a smaller home or apartment, this quality is especially helpful. Due to the small amount of oil needed, there aren't any of the intense aromas that can come from deep frying.

- **Smaller in Size**

Kitchen equipment like air fryers are comparatively small; they are a little larger than toasters. They work well in spaces where size can be an issue, like a small kitchen. They may be used in an RV or camper while travelling, as well as on a campsite, thanks to their ease of portability.

- **Reasonably Priced**

Air fryers are surprisingly affordable to purchase, especially given how practical and adaptable they are. They normally cost between £40 and £120 and are available from online retailers. However, I would advise avoiding the less expensive models and choosing quality even if it costs a bit more.

- **Simple to Use**

Most of the time, air fryers are quite simple to use and require little supervision during cooking. Simply place the food into the basket, set the timer and temperature, and let the fryer handle the rest. If you need any inspiration, there are several simple recipes available. I find frying veggies to be really simple and gratifying; the roasting effect makes the vegetables appetising.

How Do They Work?

In essence, air fryers are more intense convection ovens that are smaller and circulate hot air that has been heated by a heating element in a compact area. This heating element is located just beneath a large fan at the top, above the meal. This combination produces more intense heat in a smaller area, which cooks food more quickly than in larger, conventional ovens. Additionally, air fryers provide results that are crispier than those of an oven, making them perfect for cooking chips and other meals that require crunch.

Because of how they operate, most air fryers should be adjusted to a temperature that is 20 to 30 degrees Celsius lower than that of conventional ovens, with a 20 per cent reduction in total cooking time. This basic instruction manual was developed based on reading items like the packet instructions for standard fan ovens. There is no need to translate anything if you are using an air fryer-specific recipe, of which there are dozens online.

Almost everything may be cooked in an air fryer; then, there are certain restrictions. Even though whole chickens can be cooked with excellent, juicy results, their smaller overall size may be a challenge if, for instance, you wish to prepare a sizable dish of crispy wings.

How to Use an Air Fryer?

Although it could appear to be magic, air fryers have a straightforward mechanism. As you are aware, air fryers don't actually fry your food at all; rather, they cook it in hot oil. Instead, a fan that evenly distributes air throughout the appliance and high heat (from a coil near the food basket) provide a texture that is similar to that of deep-fried foods.

Preheat the Air Fryer

An air fryer needs time to warm before it is ready to begin cooking, much like your oven. The majority of air fryers only require a brief warm-up period, so your fryer should be ready in five minutes or less. Set the temperature of your fryer to the level at which you will be cooking (you might have a digital display or a dial to set the temperature). Some air fryers don't need to be preheated, but if you don't, your food will probably take a little longer to finish cooking. Follow the directions in your recipe for the ideal temperature to use on your fryer when you are still learning how to cook with an air fryer.

Check the Dryness of Your Food

Make careful to pat your food dry before placing it in the fryer, especially if you are frying a recipe that has a marinade. Your food will be crispier when it comes out if it is drier when it goes in. Even if you believe your ingredients are dry, give them one last pat with a paper towel before placing them in the basket because too much liquid can also result in splattering and smoking. Do not use your air fryer for cooking meals with greater fat content, such as bacon. Cooking can cause the extra fat to start smoking.

Sprinkle a Small Amount of Oil in the Basket

While we'd want to be able to fry without using any oil, air fryers do require a small amount of oil to make food crispy (albeit you will use a lot less than you would in a conventional fryer). Add your food to the air fryer basket after tossing it in a little bit of oil (about a tablespoon or less) to coat it evenly. You can also use a cooking spray with a high-smoke point that is manufactured with a healthier oil, such as avocado oil. Make sure the basket isn't packed too full of food. The nice part is that it won't get crispy if you do. To ensure that everything cooks evenly, it is recommended to cook in batches.

Air-Fry and Stir

Set the time for cooking your food according to the recipe. But don't go too far! The majority of recipes instruct you to stir your food midway through cooking or to gently shake the basket. This will aid in the even cooking and excellent, crispy cooking of everything. You might also need to check the bottom tray several times while cooking foods high in fat, such as chicken wings, to remove any extra fat. Remove the air fryer base and release the basket after the cooking period has ended. After that, take your food out of the basket and wait for it to cool before eating.

Even Cooking in an Air Fryer

It is wrong to stuff your baskets too full: In an air fryer, airflow is crucial. Therefore, even while it may be tempting to fill those baskets to the brim with fries, exercise control. A loose arrangement of the ingredients will always produce superior results, allowing the superheated convection to do its thing. Overstuffed baskets will steam rather than become crisp, and furthermore, soggy fries will not work in your favor. Do two batches in succession if you need to feed a large crowd because air fryers cook food quickly.

Packing food too tightly in the basket can limit the amount of hot air that can circulate around it and cause food to steam rather than crisp and cook unevenly. Air fryers cook food by the circulation of hot air around it. To put more food into the basket without it becoming crowded, we advise using a "jigsaw puzzle" method, chopping major proteins in half, and skewering smaller pieces of food.

Flip and Toss: Meat, poultry and seafood should be flipped midway through cooking. Although this may seem fussy, it ensures that the dish is evenly cooked. With a set of simple kitchen tongs for quick handling and to avoid reaching into a hot oven, we found it simple to accomplish this.

Toss some veggies in a bowl. Although the air fryer basket has a handle, shaking it to turn your food can result in uneven cooking. We discovered that tossing veggies, such as chips, into a bowl midway through cooking was worthwhile since it redistributed the food much more effectively for completely equal browning. (This allows you to season the food with herbs and shredded cheese around the halfway point of cooking.)

"Lincoln log" the skewers: In addition to being enjoyable to eat, kebabs offer a simple way to distribute food in the air fryer basket. In a log cabin-style layout, stacking four or more skewers perpendicularly enhanced air exposure. Our courgette fries were prepared using the same technique.

Oil-mist is a Must: You will get more of a super-dried-out coating on your food if you use no oil because air fryers cook via convection, a sort of hot air cyclone if you will. You will also note right away that hard is not the same as crisp. A tiny bit of oil will do wonders, and the dish will still be healthy because it wasn't deep fried. For a thin, even coating of the chosen oil, use an oil spray bottle. For optimal crispiness, lightly spray items with oil in your air fryer before you begin cooking them and again halfway through. Note: Avoid using aerosol cans of cooking spray because the other chemicals may result in an odd, almost plastic-like coating on the air fryer's interior and moveable parts.

Extremely light objects run the risk of damaging your fryer: The amount of extremely hot air swirling around can be devastating. Therefore, use caution even though you would think that this is a perfect opportunity to make your own tortilla chips or fried wonton strips. Light things may really be pulled into the fan if your machine doesn't have a spinning tub or enclosed basket. At best, your fan or motor will be damaged, necessitating repair or replacement. In the worst-case scenario, you might create a tiny fire within an appliance containing food that has been lightly oiled, making it less flammable than deep-fried food but still very much capable of igniting.

If you are not careful, your worktop might melt: Despite being a worktop item, air fryers emit varying degrees of heat. Check the specifications on your worktop materials to determine how they manage heat and make the necessary adjustments. I place the air fryer on a rack over a sheet pan so that air can flow underneath it and any heat may be dispersed. If your counters are laminates, the glue may melt, and prolonged heat may cause other man-made materials to sear or even shatter.

*****Notes to Remember:** Remember that foil for the kitchen has lots of wonderful uses. In order to prevent the food from sticking to the base of the fryer basket, place the foil sheet and evenly press it into the basket. Avoid lining the basket with foil when it is hot.

You could add some water to the frying tray if the air fryer is emitting white smoke. The fryer's grease may have melted, which would explain the white smoke.

If you hear noise coming from your air fryer, do not be alarmed. This is simply the sound of the fan heating the food within the fryer.

Olive oil and other oils with low smoke points should be avoided. Alternatively, if your food contains fat, make sure to cook it below the smoke point. You don't want the scent of charred food or smoking to permeate your dinnerware.

How to Clean an Air Fryer?

You will regret it if you put off cleaning. Don't let the food scraps and crumbs lie in the basket or drawer overnight; otherwise, cleaning them will be a hassle. After cooking is complete, disconnect the air fryer, let it cool, then remove the oil from the pullout drawer and discard it. When cleaning the grate, basket, and drawer after air-frying food covered in a sticky sauce, such as marinated ribs, do so while the surfaces are still warm. This will make it simpler to remove the residue. Place the removable parts in warm, soapy water to clean them. Avoid abrasives and use a soft sponge or cloth. If any of the pieces have food stuck to them, clean them after soaking them in hot water and dish soap to remove the food. Food that might be lodged in the basket or grate can be removed with a wooden skewer or toothpick. The parts should be dried individually.

A moist cloth dipped in warm, soapy water can be used to clean the interior of the air fryer. Still, the drawer and basket need to be taken out. Clean the heating element after checking for grease and food particles. Some manufacturers advise against using steel wire to remove food that has become attached to surfaces. After drying, reassemble. Dry the equipment after wiping the exterior with a moist cloth or sponge.

How Can I Get Rid of Left-over Food Odour?

Since the food is enclosed in a vessel when you are cooking in an air fryer, the odour seems to stay behind in this vessel. Even after cleaning, your air fryer may still smell strong when a food releases a strong odour when cooking. Before cleaning it once more, soak the food drawer and basket in soapy water for 30 to 60 minutes. If the fragrance still exists, cut a lemon in half, rub it over the basket and drawer, and then rewash after 30 minutes.

Be Careful with Nonstick

Customers have expressed their dissatisfaction about the nonstick coating on some air fryer parts flaking off over time on our website and in other places. Although we haven't observed this (our tests assess performance immediately out of the box), our advice for other nonstick cookware is still applicable here: Avoid using steel wool, metal utensils, or any other abrasives since they might damage the nonstick coating by scratching or chipping it. Additionally, avoid using the air fryer if the nonstick coating is peeling. Instead, make a request for a new basket over the phone from the manufacturer's customer care, or try returning the air fryer to the shop.

Air fryers let you cook with little hassle and more convenience. This compact and efficient appliance can be placed anywhere on your kitchen worktop, and all it needs is a simple plug-in to start cooking. I have been using air fryers for the past six years, and today I cook almost every other meal of the day using them. From morning frittatas to evening muffins, biscuits for kids, roasted chicken and chips, I cook them all. And now, you can also use my extensive recipe collection and enjoy all the benefits that an air fryer has to offer.

Chapter 2: Breakfast Dishes

Classic Yorkshire Puddings

SERVES: 4

PREP TIME: 20 minutes (includes 10 minutes for batter resting)
COOK TIME: 15 minutes

Ingredients:
100 g plain flour
2 large eggs
150 ml milk
½ tsp. salt
Cooking spray

Directions:
1. In a mixing bowl, whisk together the flour and salt.
2. Make a well in the centre and crack in the eggs. Gradually whisk in the milk until you have a smooth batter. Allow the batter to rest for at least 10 minutes.
3. Preheat the Air fryer to 200°C and grease 4 muffin cases with cooking spray.
4. Pour the batter evenly into the greased muffin cases, filling each about halfway.
5. Arrange the muffin cases on the Air fryer basket.
6. Bake in the air fryer for about 15 minutes, or until the Yorkshire puddings are puffed up and golden brown.
7. When cooking is complete, let the Yorkshire puddings cool slightly before serving.

British Breakfast Frittata

SERVES: 4

PREP TIME: 15 minutes
COOK TIME: 15 minutes

Ingredients:
4 large eggs
50 ml whole milk
100 g cooked bacon, chopped
1 small onion, diced
100 g cherry tomatoes, halved
50 g cheddar cheese, grated
Salt and pepper, to taste

Directions:
1. Preheat the Air fryer to 160°C.
2. In a bowl, whisk together eggs, milk, salt, and pepper.
3. Stir in the bacon, onion, tomatoes, and half the cheese.
4. Pour the mixture into a greased air fryer-safe pan and sprinkle with cheddar cheese.
5. Place the pan in the Air fryer basket. Air fry for 15 minutes.
6. When cooking is complete, serve hot.

Sizzling Bacon and Egg Muffins

SERVES: 4

Ingredients:
4 large eggs
4 slices of bacon
4 English muffins, halved
Salt and freshly ground black pepper
30 g cheddar cheese, grated

Directions:
1. Wrap each slice of bacon around the inside of a muffin case to form a ring.
2. Crack an egg into each bacon-lined case, season with salt and pepper, and sprinkle with cheese.
3. Preheat the Air fryer to 180°C.
4. Place the muffin cases in the Air fryer basket. Air fry for 10 minutes or until the eggs are set and bacon is crispy.
5. Serve hot on English muffin halves.

PREP TIME: 10 minutes
COOK TIME: 10 minutes

Crispy Black Pudding Bites

SERVES: 4

Ingredients:
200 g black pudding, sliced into 1 cm thick rounds
1 tbsp. rapeseed oil

Directions:
1. Lightly brush each slice of black pudding with rapeseed oil.
2. Preheat the Air fryer to 180°C.
3. Arrange the black pudding slices in the Air fryer basket. Air fry for 8 minutes, flipping halfway through, until crisp and heated through.
4. Serve hot, ideal as a breakfast side or snack.

PREP TIME: 5 minutes
COOK TIME: 8 minutes

Chapter 2: Breakfast Dishes / 9

Luxurious Baked Avocado Eggs

SERVES: 2

PREP TIME: 5 minutes
COOK TIME: 15 minutes

Ingredients:
2 ripe avocados, halved and pits removed
4 small eggs
Salt and freshly ground black pepper
2 tbsps. chopped chives
30 g crumbled Lancashire cheese

Directions:
1. Scoop out a bit more avocado flesh to enlarge the hole made by the pit.
2. Crack an egg into each avocado half. Season with salt and pepper.
3. Preheat the Air fryer to 190°C.
4. Place the avocado halves in a greased baking dish and then place the dish in the Air fryer basket. Bake for 15 minutes or until the eggs are set to your liking.
5. Sprinkle with chopped chives and crumbled cheese before serving.

Crispy Grilled Bacon Sandwiches

SERVES: 2

PREP TIME: 5 minutes
COOK TIME: 11 minutes

Ingredients:
4 slices of bread
8 slices of bacon
Butter, for spreading

Directions:
1. Preheat the Air fryer to 180°C.
2. Place the bacon slices in the Air fryer basket and air fry for 5 minutes until crisp. Set aside.
3. Butter the outside of each slice of bread.
4. Assemble the sandwiches with the crispy bacon.
5. Place the sandwiches in the basket and grill for about 3 minutes on each side or until the bread is toasted and golden.
6. Serve hot, cut into halves.

Sausage and Bean Breakfast Casserole

SERVES: 4

Ingredients:
4 pork sausages
1 can (400 g) baked beans
1 red pepper, diced
1 onion, diced
2 cloves garlic, minced
100 g cheddar cheese, grated
4 eggs
Salt and freshly ground black pepper

Directions:
1. Preheat the Air fryer to 200°C and grease a casserole with cooking spray.
2. Place sausages, diced pepper, onion, and garlic in the casserole. Put the casserole in the Air fryer basket and roast for 10 minutes.
3. Add baked beans to the casserole and stir to mix.
4. Make four wells in the bean mixture and crack an egg into each.
5. Sprinkle with cheese and season with salt and pepper.
6. Continue to bake for another 10 minutes or until eggs are set to your liking.
7. Serve hot, garnished with fresh parsley if desired.

PREP TIME: 10 minutes
COOK TIME: 20 minutes

Full English Breakfast Traybake

SERVES: 2

Ingredients:
4 sausages, halved
4 slices of bacon, cut into strips
100 g mushrooms, halved
1 tomato, cut into wedges
2 eggs
1 can baked beans
2 slices of bread, for toasting
Butter, for spreading
Salt and freshly ground black pepper

Directions:
1. Preheat the Air fryer to 180°C.
2. Arrange the sausages, bacon, mushrooms, and tomato wedges in the greased Air fryer basket. Air fry the ingredients for about 10-12 minutes until they are cooked through and slightly crispy, shaking the basket halfway through cooking.
3. Meanwhile, toast the bread slices and spread with butter.
4. Once the sausages, bacon, mushrooms, and tomatoes are nearly done, remove them from the Air fryer and set aside.
5. Add the baked beans to the Air fryer basket.
6. Carefully crack an egg into the basket, ensuring they don't overlap.
7. Air fry for an additional 3-5 minutes or until the eggs are cooked to your liking.
8. Season everything well with salt and pepper.
9. Serve hot alongside the toast.

PREP TIME: 5 minutes
COOK TIME: 15 minutes

Grilled Herb Mushrooms on Toast

SERVES: 2

PREP TIME: 5 minutes
COOK TIME: 8 minutes

Ingredients:
200 g chestnut mushrooms, sliced
2 tbsps. olive oil
1 clove garlic, minced
1 tsp. dried thyme
4 slices of sourdough bread
Salt and freshly ground black pepper
Cooking spray

Directions:
1. In a bowl, toss the mushrooms with olive oil, garlic, thyme, salt, and pepper.
2. Preheat the Air fryer to 180°C and grease the Air fryer basket with cooking spray.
3. Place the seasoned mushrooms in the basket and grill for 8 minutes, or until tender and slightly charred.
4. Meanwhile, toast the sourdough bread.
5. Serve the grilled mushrooms hot on the toasted sourdough bread.

Crispy Cheese and Bacon Scones

SERVES: 4

PREP TIME: 15 minutes
COOK TIME: 10 minutes

Ingredients:
225 g self-raising flour, plus extra for dusting
50 g unsalted butter, cubed
75 g sharp cheddar cheese, grated
4 slices of bacon, cooked and chopped
150 ml milk
1 tsp. English mustard
1 egg, beaten, for glazing
Salt and freshly ground black pepper
Cooking spray

Directions:
1. In a large bowl, mix the flour with a pinch of salt. Rub in the butter until the mixture resembles fine breadcrumbs.
2. Stir in the grated cheese and chopped bacon.
3. Mix the mustard with milk and gradually add to the dry ingredients, mixing until you form a soft dough.
4. Turn out onto a floured surface and gently knead just until smooth.
5. Roll out to about 2 cm thick and cut with a scone cutter.
6. Brush the tops with beaten egg.
7. Preheat the Air fryer to 200°C and grease the Air fryer basket with cooking spray.
8. Place the scones in the greased Air fryer basket and bake for 10 minutes or until risen and golden.
9. Serve warm, ideally with butter or a dollop of clotted cream.

Savoury Baked Beans on Cheesy Toast

SERVES: 2

Ingredients:
4 slices of wholemeal bread
200 g baked beans
4 slices of cheddar cheese
1 tsp. Worcestershire sauce
Butter, for spreading

Directions:
1. Butter each slice of bread and place a slice of cheese on each.
2. Preheat the Air fryer to 180°C.
3. Place the cheese-topped bread slices in the Air fryer basket and bake for 3 minutes until the cheese begins to melt.
4. Spoon baked beans over the melted cheese and drizzle with Worcestershire sauce.
5. Bake for another 5 minutes or until the beans are hot and bubbly.
6. Serve hot, ideal for a hearty breakfast or brunch.

PREP TIME: 5 minutes
COOK TIME: 8 minutes

Baked Spinach and Feta Omelette

SERVES: 2

Ingredients:
200 g fresh spinach, washed
100 g feta cheese, crumbled
4 eggs
1 tsp. nutmeg
Salt and freshly ground black pepper

Directions:
1. Preheat the Air fryer to 180°C.
2. Wilt the spinach in a pan over medium heat, then drain any excess liquid.
3. Mix the wilted spinach with nutmeg, salt, and pepper.
4. Place spinach in a greased baking dish suitable for the air fryer.
5. Sprinkle with feta cheese and create four wells in the spinach.
6. Crack an egg into each well.
7. Place the dish in the Air fryer basket and bake for 15 minutes or until eggs are set.
8. Serve warm, perfect for a nutritious start to the day.

PREP TIME: 5 minutes
COOK TIME: 15 minutes

Chapter 2: Breakfast Dishes / 13

Sumptuous Sausage and Egg Casserole

SERVES: 4

PREP TIME: 10 minutes
COOK TIME: 15 minutes

Ingredients:
200 g sausage, crumbled
4 eggs
100 ml cream
100 g cheddar cheese, grated
1 small onion, diced
Salt and freshly ground black pepper

Directions:
1. In a pan, cook the crumbled sausage and onion over medium heat until browned.
2. In a bowl, whisk together eggs, cream, salt, and pepper.
3. Stir in the cooked sausage and onion, then add the grated cheese.
4. Preheat the Air fryer to 180°C.
5. Pour the mixture into a greased air fryer-safe baking dish.
6. Arrange the dish in the Air fryer basket. Bake in the Air fryer for 15 minutes or until the casserole is set and the top is golden.
7. Serve hot, garnished with fresh herbs if desired.

Grilled Cheese and Tomato Breakfast Sandwiches

SERVES: 2

PREP TIME: 5 minutes
COOK TIME: 8 minutes

Ingredients:
4 slices of thick white bread
4 slices of cheddar cheese
1 large tomato, sliced
Butter, for spreading
Salt and freshly ground black pepper
Cooking spray

Directions:
1. Butter one side of each bread slice.
2. Layer cheese and tomato slices on the unbuttered side of two bread slices, season with salt and pepper.
3. Top with the remaining bread slices, buttered side out.
4. Preheat the Air fryer to 180°C and grease the Air fryer basket with cooking spray.
5. Grill the sandwiches in the basket for about 4 minutes per side, or until golden brown and the cheese is melted.
6. Serve hot, cut into halves or quarters.

14 \ Chapter 2: Breakfast Dishes

Chapter 3: Lunch Dishes

Modern Ploughman's Lunch

SERVES: 2

Ingredients:
2 thick slices of crusty bread
2 slices of ham
100 g cheddar cheese, sliced
1 small apple, sliced
4 pickled onions
A handful of mixed salad leaves
2 tbsps. chutney

Directions:
1. Preheat the Air fryer to 180°C.
2. Lightly butter the bread slices and put in the Air fryer basket.
3. Air fry for 5 minutes until crispy.
4. Arrange the crispy bread on plates with slices of ham, cheddar cheese, apple slices, pickled onions, salad leaves, and a dollop of chutney.
5. Serve as a hearty, quick assemble platter suitable for a refreshingly light meal.

PREP TIME: 10 minutes
COOK TIME: 5 minutes

Courgette and Ricotta Melts

SERVES: 2

Ingredients:
2 large slices of sourdough bread
1 courgette, thinly sliced
150 g ricotta cheese
Salt and freshly ground black pepper
Drizzle of olive oil
2 tsps. honey
Fresh thyme leaves
Cooking spray.

Directions:
1. Preheat the Air fryer to 180°C and grease the Air fryer basket with cooking spray.
2. Spread ricotta cheese over the bread slices and top with thinly sliced courgette.
3. Drizzle with olive oil and season with salt and pepper.
4. Place in the Air fryer basket and air fry for 8 minutes or until the edges of the bread are crispy and the courgette is tender.
5. Drizzle with honey and sprinkle fresh thyme leaves over the top before serving.

PREP TIME: 10 minutes
COOK TIME: 8 minutes

Chapter 3: Lunch Dishes / 15

Herb-Crusted Air-Fried Fish

SERVES: 2

PREP TIME: 10 minutes
COOK TIME: 12 minutes

Ingredients:
2 white fish fillets (such as cod or haddock)
1 tbsp. olive oil
50 g breadcrumbs
1 tbsp. mixed dried herbs (such as parsley, dill, and thyme)
Zest of 1 lemon
Salt and freshly ground black pepper
Cooking spray

Directions:
1. In a small bowl, mix breadcrumbs, mixed herbs, lemon zest, salt, and pepper.
2. Brush each fish fillet with olive oil, then press the breadcrumb mixture onto the top of each fillet to form a crust.
3. Preheat the Air fryer to 180°C and grease the Air fryer basket with cooking spray.
4. Place the fillets in the greased Air fryer basket, crust-side up, and air fry for 12 minutes or until the fish is cooked through and the crust is golden.
5. Serve immediately with a wedge of lemon and a side salad.

Lemon Zest Herb Chicken

SERVES: 4

PREP TIME: 10 minutes, plus 30 minutes for marinating
COOK TIME: 25 minutes

Ingredients:
4 chicken thighs
2 lemons, zest and juice
2 tbsps. olive oil
1 tbsp. mixed dried herbs (thyme, rosemary, parsley)
Salt and freshly ground black pepper
Cooking spray

Directions:
1. In a bowl, combine lemon zest, lemon juice, olive oil, mixed herbs, salt, and pepper.
2. Marinate the chicken thighs in the mixture for at least 30 minutes.
3. Preheat the Air fryer to 190°C and grease the Air fryer basket with cooking spray.
4. Place the marinated chicken thighs in the basket.
5. Roast for about 25 minutes, flipping halfway through cooking.
6. When cooking is complete, ensure the chicken is fully cooked (juices run clear) and serve hot.

Deluxe Ham and Cheese Toastie

SERVES: 2

Ingredients:
4 slices of thick bread
4 slices of ham
4 slices of cheddar cheese
Butter, for spreading
Cooking spray

PREP TIME: 5 minutes
COOK TIME: 8 minutes

Directions:
1. Butter one side of each bread slice.
2. Place a slice of cheese and a slice of ham between two slices of bread, with the buttered sides facing out.
3. Preheat the Air fryer to 180°C and grease the Air fryer basket with cooking spray.
4. Place the sandwiches in the basket.
5. Grill for about 8 minutes, flipping halfway through cooking, until the bread is golden and the cheese is melted.
6. When cooking is complete, serve hot.

Crispy Veggie Galette

SERVES: 4

Ingredients:
1 ready-rolled puff pastry
100 g cherry tomatoes, halved
1 courgette, thinly sliced
1 pepper, thinly sliced
1 red onion, thinly sliced
2 tbsps. olive oil
Salt and freshly ground black pepper
100 g feta cheese, crumbled
Fresh basil, for garnish

PREP TIME: 15 minutes
COOK TIME: 20 minutes

Directions:
1. Preheat the Air fryer to 180°C.
2. Roll out the puff pastry and lightly press into a greased, air fryer-safe pie or tart pan.
3. Toss the vegetables in olive oil, salt, and pepper and arrange them on the pastry. Crumble feta cheese on top.
4. Place the pan in the Air fryer basket and bake for 20 minutes or until the pastry is golden and vegetables are roasted.
5. Garnish with fresh basil before serving.

Chapter 3: Lunch Dishes / 17

Quick Shepherd's Pie

SERVES: 4

PREP TIME: 20 minutes
COOK TIME: 15 minutes

Ingredients:
300 g minced lamb
1 onion, chopped
2 carrots, diced
2 cloves garlic, minced
1 tbsp. tomato purée
300 ml beef or lamb stock
1 tsp. Worcestershire sauce
500 g mashed potatoes
50 g cheddar cheese, grated
Salt and freshly ground black pepper

Directions:
1. In a frying pan over medium-high heat, brown the lamb with onions, carrots, and garlic. Stir in the tomato purée, stock, and Worcestershire sauce. Simmer until thickened, then season with salt and pepper.
2. Transfer the lamb mixture into a greased, air fryer-safe baking dish.
3. Top with mashed potatoes and sprinkle with grated cheese.
4. Preheat the Air fryer to 180°C.
5. Place the baking dish in the Air fryer basket. Bake for 15 minutes or until the top is golden and crispy.
6. Serve hot, garnished with fresh herbs if desired.

Smoky Kippers and Eggs

SERVES: 2

PREP TIME: 5 minutes
COOK TIME: 8 minutes

Ingredients:
2 kippers
2 eggs
1 tbsp. butter
Fresh parsley, chopped for garnish
Pepper, to taste
Cooking spray

Directions:
1. Preheat the Air fryer to 180°C and grease the Air fryer basket with cooking spray.
2. Place the kippers in the basket and air fry for about 4 minutes.
3. Crack an egg over each kipper, add a dollop of butter on top, and continue to air fry for another 4 minutes or until the eggs are cooked to your preference.
4. When cooking is complete, season with pepper and garnish with fresh parsley. Serve hot.

Chapter 3: Lunch Dishes

Asparagus and Parma Ham Spirals

SERVES: 4

Ingredients:
12 asparagus spears, trimmed
12 slices of Parma ham
Olive oil, for drizzling
Freshly ground black pepper
Cooking spray

Directions:
1. Wrap each asparagus spear with a slice of Parma ham.
2. Drizzle with a little olive oil and season with black pepper.
3. Preheat the Air fryer to 180°C and grease the Air fryer basket with cooking spray.
4. Place the wrapped asparagus in the basket.
5. Air fry for about 10 minutes, until the asparagus is tender and the Parma ham is crispy.
6. When cooking is complete, serve hot.

PREP TIME: 5 minutes
COOK TIME: 10 minutes

Orchard Pork Sausages with Rustic Mash

SERVES: 2

Ingredients:
4 pork and apple sausages
4 large potatoes, peeled and chopped
50 ml milk
2 tbsps. butter
1 tbsp. wholemeal mustard
Salt and freshly ground black pepper
Cooking spray

Directions:
1. Preheat the Air fryer to 180°C and grease the Air fryer basket with cooking spray.
2. Place the sausages in the greased Air fryer basket.
3. Air fry the sausages for about 10 minutes, flipping halfway through.
4. Meanwhile, boil the potatoes until tender, then drain.
5. Mash the potatoes with milk, butter, mustard, salt, and pepper until smooth.
6. Serve the sausages hot with the rustic mustard mash.

PREP TIME: 15 minutes
COOK TIME: 20 minutes

Chapter 3: Lunch Dishes / 19

Pub-Style Beef and Ale Hand Pies

SERVES: 4

PREP TIME: 30 minutes
COOK TIME: 20 minutes

Ingredients:
300 g chuck steak, diced
1 onion, finely chopped
2 cloves garlic, minced
200 ml ale
1 tbsp. Worcestershire sauce
1 beef stock cube
2 tbsps. flour
1 roll shortcrust pastry
1 egg, beaten for egg wash
Salt and freshly ground black pepper
Cooking spray

Directions:
1. In a pan over medium heat, brown the beef with onions and garlic. Sprinkle over the flour and stir until well coated.
2. Add the ale, Worcestershire sauce, crumbled stock cube, and bring to a simmer until the sauce thickens and the beef is tender.
3. Allow the filling to cool slightly, then spoon into circles of shortcrust pastry, fold over, and seal the edges.
4. Brush with egg wash.
5. Preheat the Air fryer to 180°C and grease the Air fryer basket with cooking spray.
6. Place the pies in the basket and bake for 20 minutes or until golden and crisp.
7. Serve hot, ideal with a side of mashed potatoes or peas.

Luxurious Welsh Rarebit Toasts

SERVES: 2

PREP TIME: 5 minutes
COOK TIME: 10 minutes

Ingredients:
2 large slices of crusty bread
150 g mature cheddar, grated
1 tsp. English mustard
1 tbsp. Worcestershire sauce
2 tbsps. beer (optional)
1 tbsp. flour
1 egg yolk
Pepper, to taste
Cooking spray

Directions:
1. In a bowl, mix the cheese, mustard, Worcestershire sauce, beer, flour, and egg yolk to form a thick paste.
2. Spread this mixture on the slices of bread.
3. Preheat the Air fryer to 180°C and grease the Air fryer basket with cooking spray.
4. Place the prepared slices in the basket and grill for about 10 minutes or until the topping is bubbling and golden.
5. When cooking is complete, serve hot, sprinkled with black pepper.

Minty Air Fried Lamb Chops

SERVES: 2

Ingredients:
4 lamb chops
2 tbsps. olive oil
Salt and freshly ground black pepper
For the Mint Sauce:
10 g fresh mint, finely chopped
2 tbsps. malt vinegar
1 tbsp. sugar
Pinch of salt
Cooking spray

PREP TIME: 10 minutes
COOK TIME: 12 minutes

Directions:
1. Preheat the Air fryer to 200°C and grease the Air fryer basket with cooking spray.
2. Rub the lamb chops with olive oil, salt, and pepper.
3. Place the lamb chops in the basket and air fry for about 6 minutes per side or until they reach desired doneness.
4. Meanwhile, mix the mint, vinegar, sugar, and salt in a small bowl to create the mint sauce.
5. Serve the lamb chops hot, drizzled with the mint sauce.

Cheesy Onion Pie

SERVES: 4

Ingredients:
1 roll shortcrust pastry
3 large onions, thinly sliced
2 tbsps. butter
200 g mature cheddar cheese, grated
100 ml cream
2 eggs
Salt and freshly ground black pepper
1 egg, beaten for egg wash

PREP TIME: 20 minutes
COOK TIME: 20 minutes

Directions:
1. In a pan over medium-low heat, melt butter and gently cook the onions until soft and translucent.
2. In a bowl, whisk together eggs, cream, salt, and pepper.
3. Stir the cooked onions and grated cheese into the egg mixture.
4. Roll out the pastry and line a greased, air fryer-safe pie dish.
5. Pour the onion and cheese mixture into the pastry shell.
6. Brush the edges of the pastry with egg wash.
7. Preheat the Air fryer to 180°C.
8. Arrange the pie dish in the Air fryer basket. Bake the pie in the air fryer for 20 minutes or until the filling is set and the pastry is golden.
9. Serve hot, perfect as a hearty lunch or dinner.

Chapter 4: Dinner Dishes

Grilled Gammon with Garden Peas and Silky Hollandaise

SERVES: 2

PREP TIME: 10 minutes
COOK TIME: 15 minutes

Ingredients:
2 gammon steaks
200 g frozen garden peas
2 eggs
For the Hollandaise:
2 egg yolks
1 tbsp. lemon juice
100 g unsalted butter, melted
Salt and cayenne pepper to taste
Cooking spray

Directions:
1. Preheat the Air fryer to 200°C and grease the Air fryer basket with cooking spray.
2. Place the gammon steaks in the basket and grill for about 12 minutes, flipping halfway through.
3. Meanwhile, cook the peas in boiling water for about 5 minutes until tender.
4. For the Hollandaise, blend egg yolks and lemon juice. Slowly add melted butter until the sauce thickens. Season with salt and cayenne.
5. Poach eggs in simmering water until the whites are set but yolks remain runny.
6. Serve the grilled gammon with peas, a poached egg on top, and drizzle with Hollandaise sauce.

Ale-Braised Beef Brisket

SERVES: 4

PREP TIME: 15 minutes
COOK TIME: 60 minutes

Ingredients:
1 kg beef brisket, trimmed
2 onions, sliced
2 cloves garlic, minced
500 ml ale
2 tbsps. Worcestershire sauce
Salt and freshly ground black pepper
2 tbsps. fresh thyme

Directions:
1. Season the brisket with salt, pepper, and thyme.
2. Preheat the Air fryer to 160°C.
3. Place brisket in a greased, air fryer-safe dish, top with onions and garlic, and pour over the ale and Worcestershire sauce.
4. Cover the dish with foil and arrange in the Air fryer basket. Bake in the air fryer for 60 minutes, or until the meat is tender.
5. Slice the brisket and serve with the cooking juices as a gravy.

Duck with Orange Sauce

SERVES: 2

Ingredients:
1 whole duck (approximately 1.5 kg), trimmed and scored
Salt and freshly ground black pepper
For the Orange Sauce:
Juice and zest of 2 oranges
2 tbsps. honey
1 tbsp. soy sauce
1 clove garlic, minced
1 tsp. ginger, grated
100 ml chicken stock
Cooking spray

PREP TIME: 15 minutes
COOK TIME: 60 minutes

Directions:
1. Season the duck generously with salt and pepper.
2. Preheat the Air fryer to 180°C and lightly grease the Air fryer basket with cooking spray.
3. Place the duck breast-side down in the basket and roast for 30 minutes. Flip the duck and continue cooking for another 20-30 minutes, or until the skin is crispy and the internal temperature reaches 74°C.
4. For the sauce, combine orange juice and zest, honey, soy sauce, garlic, ginger, and chicken stock in a small saucepan. Simmer over medium heat until reduced and thickened.
5. Serve the duck sliced with the citrus-infused orange sauce drizzled over the top.

Thai Coconut Chilli Chicken

SERVES: 4

Ingredients:
4 chicken breasts
1 can coconut milk
2 tbsps. peanut butter
1 tbsp. chilli flakes
1 tbsp. soy sauce
1 tbsp. honey
2 cloves garlic, minced
1 lime, juiced
Fresh coriander, chopped for garnish
Salt and pepper to taste
Cooking spray

PREP TIME: 15 minutes, plus 30 minutes for marinating
COOK TIME: 20 minutes

Directions:
1. In a bowl, mix together coconut milk, peanut butter, chilli flakes, soy sauce, honey, garlic, and lime juice to create a marinade. Season with salt and pepper.
2. Marinate the chicken breasts in the mixture for at least 30 minutes.
3. Preheat the Air fryer to 180°C and grease the Air fryer basket with cooking spray.
4. Place the marinated chicken in the basket and bake for 20 minutes or until the chicken is cooked through.
5. Garnish with fresh coriander and serve hot.

Chapter 4: Dinner Dishes / 23

Barbecue Pork Belly

SERVES: 4

PREP TIME: 10 minutes
COOK TIME: 30 minutes

Ingredients:
800 g pork belly, scored
2 tbsps. barbecue seasoning
2 tbsps. olive oil
Salt and freshly ground black pepper

Directions:
1. Rub the pork belly with olive oil, barbecue seasoning, salt, and pepper.
2. Preheat the Air fryer to 180°C.
3. Place the pork belly in the Air fryer basket, skin-side up.
4. Air fry for 30 minutes or until the pork is tender and the skin is crispy.
5. Let rest for a few minutes before slicing. Serve hot with additional barbecue sauce if desired.

Herb-Crusted Sea Bream

SERVES: 2

PREP TIME: 10 minutes
COOK TIME: 15 minutes

Ingredients:
2 sea bream fillets
100 g samphire, washed
2 tbsps. olive oil
1 tbsp. mixed dried herbs
Salt and freshly ground black pepper
Lemon slices for garnish
Cooking spray

Directions:
1. Brush the sea bream fillets with olive oil and season with mixed herbs, salt, and pepper.
2. Preheat the Air fryer to 180°C and grease the Air fryer basket with cooking spray.
3. Lay the samphire at the bottom of the basket, and place the seasoned fillets on top.
4. Bake for 15 minutes or until the fish is cooked through and flaky.
5. Serve the sea bream on a bed of samphire, garnished with lemon slices.

24 \ Chapter 4: Dinner Dishes

Lamb Shoulder Feast with Peppered Rosemary Jus

SERVES: 4

PREP TIME: 20 minutes
COOK TIME: 60 minutes

Ingredients:
1 lamb shoulder, about 1.5 kg
2 red peppers, sliced
4 cloves garlic, minced
Fresh rosemary
Salt and freshly ground black pepper
500 ml lamb stock
Cooking spray

Directions:
1. Rub the lamb shoulder with garlic, rosemary, salt, and pepper.
2. Preheat the Air fryer to 180°C and grease the Air fryer basket with cooking spray.
3. Place the lamb in the Air fryer basket and surround with sliced peppers.
4. Roast for 60 minutes or until the lamb is tender and the peppers are charred.
5. Remove the lamb and let rest. Simmer the collected juices and peppers with lamb stock in a pan to make a rosemary jus.
6. Carve the lamb and serve with the rosemary jus.

Parsnip and White Wine Guinea Fowl

SERVES: 2

PREP TIME: 15 minutes
COOK TIME: 25 minutes

Ingredients:
1 guinea fowl, cut into pieces
1 parsnip, sliced
2 shallots, sliced
200 ml white wine
2 tbsps. olive oil
Salt and freshly ground black pepper
Fresh herbs for garnish
Cooking spray

Directions:
1. Season the guinea fowl pieces with salt and pepper and rub with olive oil.
2. Preheat the Air fryer to 180°C and grease a baking dish with cooking spray.
3. Place the fowl, parsnip, and shallots in the greased dish. Arrange the dish in the Air fryer basket and roast for 20 minutes.
4. Pour the white wine over the guinea fowl and continue to roast for an additional 5 minutes, or until the fowl is cooked through and vegetables are tender.
5. Serve garnished with fresh herbs, ideally with a side of roasted potatoes.

Whisky Glazed Short Ribs

SERVES: 4

PREP TIME: 20 minutes
COOK TIME: 35 minutes

Ingredients:
800 g beef short ribs
240 ml beef broth
120 ml Scotch whisky or red wine
2 tbsps. tomato purée
1 onion, chopped
2 carrots, chopped
2 cloves garlic, minced
2 tbsps. olive oil
Salt and freshly ground black pepper
Fresh parsley, chopped for garnish

Directions:
1. Season the short ribs with salt and pepper.
2. Preheat the Air fryer to 160°C.
3. In a bowl, mix beef broth, Scotch whisky, and tomato purée.
4. Place the short ribs in a greased, air fryer-safe baking dish and top with onions, carrots, and garlic. Pour the broth mixture over the ribs.
5. Arrange the baking dish in the Air fryer basket. Roast for 35 minutes, turning the ribs halfway through.
6. Garnish with fresh parsley and serve with mashed potatoes or crusty bread.

Lemon-Thyme Roasted Chicken

SERVES: 4

PREP TIME: 10 minutes
COOK TIME: 50 minutes

Ingredients:
1 whole chicken (about 1.5 kg)
2 lemons, one sliced and one juiced
4 sprigs of thyme
3 tbsps. olive oil
Salt and freshly ground black pepper
1 garlic bulb, halved
Cooking spray

Directions:
1. Rub the chicken with olive oil, lemon juice, salt, and pepper. Place lemon slices and thyme inside the cavity.
2. Preheat the Air fryer to 200°C and grease the Air fryer basket with cooking spray.
3. Place the chicken in the basket and add the garlic bulb halves around it.
4. Roast for 50 minutes, or until the chicken is golden and the juices run clear.
5. Rest the chicken for 10 minutes before carving. Serve with the roasted garlic and additional fresh thyme.

Chapter 4: Dinner Dishes

Dill and Lemon Infused Salmon

SERVES: 2

Ingredients:
2 salmon fillets
2 tbsps. olive oil
1 lemon, zested and juiced
2 tbsps. fresh dill, chopped
Salt and freshly ground black pepper
Cooking spray

Directions:
1. Combine olive oil, lemon zest, lemon juice, and dill in a small bowl. Season with salt and pepper.
2. Brush the salmon fillets with the lemon-dill mixture.
3. Preheat the Air fryer to 180°C and grease the Air fryer basket with cooking spray.
4. Place the salmon in the basket and bake for 15 minutes, or until the salmon is cooked through and flakes easily.
5. Serve the salmon with a side of steamed vegetables or a fresh salad.

PREP TIME: 5 minutes
COOK TIME: 15 minutes

Colourful Stuffed Pepper Medley

SERVES: 4

Ingredients:
4 peppers, tops cut off and seeds removed
200 g cooked rice
100 g feta cheese, crumbled
100 g black olives, chopped
1 small red onion, finely diced
2 tomatoes, diced
2 cloves garlic, minced
1 tsp. dried oregano
Salt and freshly ground black pepper
1 tsp. olive oil
Cooking spray

Directions:
1. In a bowl, mix the cooked rice, feta cheese, olives, onion, tomatoes, garlic, and oregano. Season with salt and pepper.
2. Drizzle the inside of the peppers with olive oil and fill each with the rice mixture.
3. Preheat the Air fryer to 180°C and grease the Air fryer basket with cooking spray.
4. Place the stuffed peppers in the basket and bake for 20 minutes or until the peppers are tender and the filling is hot.
5. Serve hot, garnished with fresh herbs if desired.

PREP TIME: 15 minutes
COOK TIME: 20 minutes

Satay Roast Chicken

SERVES: 4

PREP TIME: 20 minutes, plus 30 minutes for marinating
COOK TIME: 30 minutes

Ingredients:
4 chicken breasts
2 tbsps. peanut butter
1 tbsp. soy sauce
1 tbsp. honey
1 tsp. curry powder
1 clove garlic, minced
1 tbsp. lime juice
Salt to taste
Chopped peanuts and fresh coriander for garnish
Cooking spray

Directions:
1. In a bowl, combine peanut butter, soy sauce, honey, curry powder, garlic, lime juice, and salt to make the marinade.
2. Coat the chicken breasts in the marinade and let sit for at least 30 minutes.
3. Preheat the Air fryer to 180°C and grease the Air fryer basket with cooking spray.
4. Place the marinated chicken breasts in the basket.
5. Roast for 30 minutes or until the chicken is golden and cooked through.
6. Serve garnished with chopped peanuts and coriander.

Orchard Roast Pork with Cider Apples

SERVES: 4

PREP TIME: 20 minutes
COOK TIME: 60 minutes

Ingredients:
1 kg pork loin roast
4 apples, quartered
2 onions, quartered
2 tbsps. olive oil
1 tsp. salt
½ tsp. freshly ground black pepper
1 tsp. thyme
200 ml apple cider

Directions:
1. Preheat the Air fryer to 180°C.
2. Rub the pork loin with olive oil, salt, pepper, and thyme.
3. Place the pork in the Air fryer basket. Surround it with apple and onion quarters.
4. Roast for 60 minutes, or until the pork is fully cooked and the apples and onions are caramelised.
5. While the pork is resting, pour the apple cider into a small saucepan. Heat the cider over medium heat until it reduces by half, creating a glaze.
6. Let the roast rest for 10 minutes before slicing. Serve with the roasted apples and onions, drizzling the reduced apple cider glaze and any cooking juices over the top.

Chapter 4: Dinner Dishes

Chapter 5: Vegan and Vegetarian Dishes

Toasted Sourdough and Hazelnut Asparagus

SERVES: 2

Ingredients:
200 g fresh asparagus, trimmed
50 g hazelnuts, chopped
50 g sourdough breadcrumbs
2 tbsps. olive oil
Salt and freshly ground black pepper
Cooking spray

PREP TIME: 5 minutes
COOK TIME: 10 minutes

Directions:
1. Preheat the Air fryer to 200°C and grease the Air fryer basket with cooking spray.
2. In a bowl, mix the chopped hazelnuts and sourdough breadcrumbs with olive oil, salt, and pepper.
3. Lay the asparagus in the greased Air fryer basket.
4. Sprinkle the breadcrumb and hazelnut mixture over the asparagus.
5. Roast for 10 minutes, or until the asparagus is tender and the topping is golden and crispy.
6. Serve hot, perfect as a side dish or a light meal.

Marmite and Poppy Seed Parsnips

SERVES: 4

Ingredients:
4 large parsnips, peeled and quartered
1 tbsp. Marmite
2 tbsps. olive oil
1 tbsp. poppy seeds
Salt to taste
Cooking spray

PREP TIME: 5 minutes
COOK TIME: 15 minutes

Directions:
1. In a large bowl, mix Marmite, olive oil, and a pinch of salt until well combined.
2. Toss the parsnips in the Marmite mixture until evenly coated.
3. Preheat the Air fryer to 190°C and grease the Air fryer basket with cooking spray.
4. Lay the coated parsnips in the basket and sprinkle with poppy seeds.
5. Roast for 15 minutes, or until the parsnips are golden and tender.
6. Serve hot, ideal as a savoury, flavourful side dish.

Pear and Chestnut Festive Stuffing

SERVES: 4

PREP TIME: 10 minutes
COOK TIME: 20 minutes

Ingredients:
2 onions, thinly sliced
2 pears, cored and chopped
100 g cooked chestnuts, chopped
100 g dried breadcrumbs
50 g butter
1 tsp. thyme
Salt and freshly ground black pepper

Directions:
1. Melt the butter in a pan over medium heat and sauté the onions until caramelised.
2. Add the chopped pears and cook until soft.
3. In a bowl, mix the caramelised onion and pear mixture with chestnuts, breadcrumbs, thyme, salt, and pepper.
4. Transfer the mixture into a greased baking dish suitable for the air fryer.
5. Preheat the Air fryer to 160°C.
6. Arrange the baking dish in the Air fryer basket. Bake for 20 minutes or until the top is crispy and golden.
7. Serve hot, perfect for accompanying a roast or as a festive side dish.

Golden Honey-Tahini Cauliflower

SERVES: 4

PREP TIME: 10 minutes
COOK TIME: 20 minutes

Ingredients:
1 large cauliflower, cut into florets
3 tbsps. tahini
2 tbsps. honey
1 tbsp. olive oil
Salt and pepper to taste
For the Pilau Rice:
200 g basmati rice, rinsed
350 ml vegetable broth
50 g dried apricots, chopped
50 g raisins
2 tbsps. pistachios, chopped
1 tsp. turmeric
1 tsp. cumin
Salt to taste
Cooking spray

Directions:
1. Mix tahini, honey, olive oil, salt, and pepper in a bowl. Toss cauliflower florets in the mixture until well coated.
2. Preheat the Air fryer to 200°C and grease the Air fryer basket with cooking spray.
3. Spread the cauliflower florets in the basket and roast for 20 minutes or until golden and tender.
4. Meanwhile, cook the rice with broth, turmeric, and cumin until fluffy. Stir in apricots, raisins, and pistachios.
5. Serve the roasted cauliflower over the jewelled pilau rice, garnished with extra pistachios if desired.

Chapter 5: Vegan and Vegetarian Dishes

Spiced Aloo Tikki Bites

SERVES: 4

Ingredients:
500 g potatoes, boiled and mashed
1 tsp. cumin seeds
½ tsp. ground coriander
½ tsp. turmeric
½ tsp. smoked paprika
2 tbsps. fresh parsley, chopped
1 small leek, finely chopped
Salt and pepper to taste
2 tbsps. oil for brushing
Cooking spray

PREP TIME: 20 minutes
COOK TIME: 10 minutes

Directions:
1. In a bowl, combine mashed potatoes, cumin seeds, ground coriander, turmeric, smoked paprika, chopped parsley, chopped leek, and season with salt and pepper.
2. Form the potato mixture into small patties.
3. Preheat the Air fryer to 200°C and grease the Air fryer basket with cooking spray.
4. Place the patties in the basket, brush with oil, and cook for 10 minutes, flipping halfway through, until golden and crispy.
5. Serve hot with a side of minted yoghurt or a simple tomato chutney.

Healthy Wholemeal Loaf

SERVES: 4

Ingredients:
500 g wholemeal flour
7 g dried yeast
1 tsp. salt
1 tbsp. honey
300 ml warm water

PREP TIME: 15 minutes, plus 1 hour proofing time
COOK TIME: 25 minutes

Directions:
1. In a large bowl, mix wholemeal flour, yeast, and salt.
2. Stir in honey and warm water to form a dough.
3. Knead the dough on a floured surface for about 10 minutes until smooth and elastic.
4. Let the dough rise in a warm place until doubled in size, about 1 hour.
5. Punch down the dough and shape it into a loaf.
6. Place the dough in a greased air fryer-safe loaf pan.
7. Preheat the Air fryer to 180°C.
8. Arrange the pan in the Air fryer basket. Bake for 25 minutes or until the loaf is golden and sounds hollow when tapped.
9. Let cool slightly before slicing. Serve warm with butter or jam.

Chapter 5: Vegan and Vegetarian Dishes / 31

Balsamic Glazed Tofu and Gnocchi

SERVES: 2

PREP TIME: 10 minutes
COOK TIME: 20 minutes

Ingredients:
300 g tofu, pressed and cubed
300 g potato gnocchi
3 tbsps. balsamic vinegar
2 tbsps. olive oil
1 tsp. dried basil
1 tsp. garlic powder
Salt and freshly ground black pepper
Fresh basil, for garnish
Cooking spray

Directions:
1. In a bowl, mix balsamic vinegar, olive oil, dried basil, garlic powder, salt, and pepper.
2. Toss the tofu and gnocchi in the balsamic mixture until well coated.
3. Preheat the Air fryer to 200°C and grease the Air fryer basket with cooking spray.
4. Spread the tofu and gnocchi evenly in the basket.
5. Air fry for 20 minutes, stirring halfway through, until the gnocchi is golden and the tofu is crispy.
6. Serve hot, garnished with fresh basil leaves.

Satay-Style Whole Cauliflower

SERVES: 4

PREP TIME: 10 minutes
COOK TIME: 30 minutes

Ingredients:
1 whole cauliflower
3 tbsps. peanut butter
2 tbsps. soy sauce
1 tbsp. lime juice
1 tbsp. honey
1 tsp. chilli flakes
1 clove garlic, minced
Water as needed to thin the sauce
Fresh coriander for garnish
Cooking spray

Directions:
1. Trim the cauliflower leaves and core so it sits flat.
2. Mix peanut butter, soy sauce, lime juice, honey, chilli flakes, and garlic in a bowl. Thin with water to a pourable consistency.
3. Brush the entire cauliflower with the satay sauce.
4. Preheat the Air fryer to 180°C and grease the Air fryer basket with cooking spray.
5. Place the cauliflower in the Air fryer basket. Roast for 30 minutes or until the surface is crispy and the cauliflower is tender.
6. Garnish with fresh coriander and serve as a striking centrepiece.

Veggie Moussaka

SERVES: 4

Ingredients:
- 2 large aubergines, sliced into rounds
- 2 large potatoes, sliced into rounds
- 200 g canned tomatoes
- 1 onion, chopped
- 2 cloves garlic, minced
- 100 g feta cheese, crumbled (optional for vegan version)

For the Béchamel Sauce:
- 50 g flour
- 50 g butter or vegan butter
- 500 ml milk or plant-based milk
- Nutmeg, grated
- Salt and pepper to taste

PREP TIME: 30 minutes
COOK TIME: 40 minutes

Directions:
1. Salt the aubergine and potato slices and set aside for 30 minutes to draw out moisture. Rinse and pat dry.
2. Sauté the chopped onion and minced garlic in a pan until softened, about 5 minutes.
3. Layer aubergine and potato slices in a greased air fryer-safe dish, alternating with sautéed onions, garlic, and tomatoes.
4. Prepare béchamel sauce by melting butter, whisking in flour, gradually adding milk, and cooking until thickened. Season with nutmeg, salt, and pepper.
5. Pour béchamel sauce over the vegetable layers and top with crumbled feta.
6. Preheat the Air fryer to 180°C.
7. Put the dish in the Air fryer basket. Bake for 35 minutes or until the top is golden and bubbling.
8. Let cool slightly before serving, allowing layers to set.

Beetroot and Lentil Veggie Burgers

SERVES: 4

Ingredients:
- 200 g cooked beetroot, grated
- 150 g cooked lentils
- 1 onion, finely chopped
- 2 cloves garlic, minced
- 100 g breadcrumbs
- 1 egg (or flax egg for vegan version)
- 1 tsp. smoked paprika
- Salt and freshly ground black pepper
- Oil for brushing
- Cooking spray

PREP TIME: 15 minutes
COOK TIME: 10 minutes

Directions:
1. In a large bowl, mix together beetroot, lentils, onion, garlic, breadcrumbs, egg, smoked paprika, salt, and pepper. Form into patties.
2. Preheat the Air fryer to 200°C and lightly grease the Air fryer basket with cooking spray.
3. Place the patties in the basket, brush with oil, and air fry for about 10 minutes, flipping halfway through until they are firm and nicely charred.
4. Serve hot in burger buns with your favourite toppings.

Chapter 5: Vegan and Vegetarian Dishes / 33

Savoury Nut Carrot Bites

SERVES: 4

PREP TIME: 15 minutes
COOK TIME: 20 minutes

Ingredients:
150 g mixed nuts, finely chopped
100 g breadcrumbs
1 onion, finely chopped
2 cloves garlic, minced
1 carrot, grated
100 g mushrooms, finely chopped
2 eggs, beaten
2 tbsps. soy sauce
1 tbsp. Worcestershire sauce (vegetarian)
Fresh herbs (thyme, rosemary), chopped
Salt and pepper to taste
For the Onion Gravy:
1 onion, sliced
2 tbsps. flour
500 ml vegetable stock
1 tsp. balsamic vinegar

Directions:
1. Preheat the Air fryer to 180°C.
2. Combine nuts, breadcrumbs, vegetables, eggs, soy sauce, Worcestershire sauce, herbs, salt, and pepper in a bowl. Mix thoroughly.
3. Form into balls and place in a greased Air fryer basket.
4. Air fry for 20 minutes or until firm and golden.
5. For the gravy, sauté the onion in a frying pan over medium heat until soft. Stir in the flour, then slowly add the stock and vinegar, simmering until thickened.
6. Serve the nut roast bites with onion gravy and steamed greens.

Cider-Braised Veggie Sausage Hotpot

SERVES: 4

PREP TIME: 10 minutes
COOK TIME: 20 minutes

Ingredients:
4 vegetarian sausages
2 apples, cored and sliced
1 onion, sliced
2 cloves garlic, minced
300 ml apple cider
1 tbsp. wholemeal mustard
Fresh thyme
Salt and freshly ground black pepper
1 tbsp. oil
Cooking spray

Directions:
1. Preheat the Air fryer to 180°C and grease the casserole with cooking spray.
2. Place sausages, apples, onion, and garlic in the casserole. Drizzle with oil and cider, then sprinkle with mustard, thyme, salt, and pepper.
3. Arrange the casserole in the Air fryer basket. Bake for 20 minutes until cooked through.
4. Serve hot, garnished with additional thyme.

Herbed Polenta and Mushroom Bake

SERVES: 4

Ingredients:
200 g polenta
600 ml vegetable broth
100 g grated cheese (use vegan cheese for a vegan version)
200 g mushrooms, sliced
1 can chickpeas, drained and rinsed
3 cloves garlic, minced
50 g butter (or vegan butter)
Salt and freshly ground black pepper
Fresh parsley, chopped for garnish

PREP TIME: 15 minutes
COOK TIME: 25 minutes

Directions:
1. Cook polenta in vegetable broth according to package instructions until thick and creamy. Stir in half of the cheese.
2. In a frying pan over medium heat, cook the mushrooms, chickpeas, and garlic in butter until mushrooms are golden.
3. Layer the cooked polenta in a greased air fryer-safe dish, top with the mushroom mixture, and sprinkle with the remaining cheese.
4. Preheat the Air fryer to 180°C.
5. Place the dish in the Air fryer basket. Bake for 25 minutes, or until the top is golden and bubbly.
6. Garnish with fresh parsley before serving.

Summer Vegetable Gratin

SERVES: 4

Ingredients:
2 courgettes, sliced
2 yellow courgettes, sliced
1 aubergine, sliced
1 red pepper, sliced
200 g ricotta cheese
200 ml tomato sauce
100 g grated mozzarella cheese
2 cloves garlic, minced
1 tbsp. olive oil
Salt and freshly ground black pepper
Fresh basil, for garnish

PREP TIME: 20 minutes
COOK TIME: 30 minutes

Directions:
1. In a bowl, toss the sliced vegetables with olive oil, garlic, salt, and pepper.
2. Layer half of the vegetables in a greased air fryer-safe baking dish.
3. Spread ricotta cheese and half of the tomato sauce over the vegetables.
4. Add another layer of vegetables, top with the remaining tomato sauce, and sprinkle with mozzarella.
5. Preheat the Air fryer to 180°C.
6. Arrange the baking dish in the Air fryer basket. Bake for 30 minutes, or until the vegetables are tender and the cheese is bubbly and golden.
7. Garnish with fresh basil leaves before serving.

Chapter 5: Vegan and Vegetarian Dishes

Chapter 6: Snacks and Starters

Feta and Honey Filo Parcels

SERVES: 4

PREP TIME: 15 minutes
COOK TIME: 12 minutes

Ingredients:
200 g feta cheese, cut into 8 pieces
8 sheets filo pastry
50 g butter, melted
2 tbsps. honey
1 tsp. ground cinnamon
1 tsp. sesame seeds
Fresh mint, for garnish
Cooking spray

Directions:
1. Preheat the Air fryer to 180°C.
2. Brush each filo sheet with melted butter.
3. Place a piece of feta at one end of each filo sheet, fold the sides over the feta, and roll up into parcels.
4. Grease the Air fryer basket with cooking spray.
5. Place the parcels in the basket, seam side down.
6. Air fry for 12 minutes or until golden and crispy.
7. Meanwhile, warm the honey and mix with ground cinnamon.
8. Drizzle the spiced honey over the filo parcels, sprinkle with sesame seeds, and garnish with fresh mint before serving.

Golden Air-Fried Scotch Eggs

SERVES: 4

PREP TIME: 20 minutes
COOK TIME: 15 minutes

Ingredients:
4 large eggs
400 g sausage meat
1 tbsp. fresh parsley, chopped
1 tsp. English mustard
120 g plain flour
2 eggs, beaten
120 g breadcrumbs
Salt and freshly ground black pepper
Cooking spray

Directions:
1. Place the 4 large eggs in a saucepan of boiling water and cook for 6 minutes. Transfer the eggs to a bowl of cold water to cool. Once cooled, peel the eggs.
2. In a mixing bowl, combine the sausage meat, parsley, mustard, salt, and pepper. Divide the mixture into 4 equal portions.
3. Flatten each portion of the sausage mixture into a patty and wrap it around each peeled egg, ensuring the egg is completely covered.
4. Prepare three separate bowls: one with flour, one with beaten eggs, and one with breadcrumbs. Roll each sausage-wrapped egg in flour, then dip in beaten eggs, and finally roll in breadcrumbs to coat evenly.
5. Preheat the Air fryer to 200°C and grease the Air fryer basket with cooking spray.
6. Place the coated Scotch eggs in the Air fryer basket, ensuring they are not touching.
7. Air fry for 15 minutes, flipping halfway through cooking for even browning.
8. Serve the Scotch eggs hot, optionally with a side of mustard or your favourite dipping sauce.

Creamy Boursin-Stuffed Mushrooms

SERVES: 4

Ingredients:
Cooking spray
12 large button mushrooms, stems removed
150 g Boursin cheese
120 g breadcrumbs
1 tbsp. olive oil
Fresh parsley, chopped, for garnish

PREP TIME: 10 minutes
COOK TIME: 10 minutes

Directions:
1. Clean the mushrooms and remove the stems. Pat them dry with a paper towel.
2. In a small bowl, combine the Boursin cheese with the breadcrumbs and olive oil until well mixed.
3. Fill each mushroom cap with the breadcrumb and Boursin cheese mixture using a spoon.
4. Preheat the Air fryer to 180°C and grease the Air fryer basket with cooking spray.
5. Place the stuffed mushrooms in the Air fryer basket in a single layer.
6. Air fry for 10 minutes or until the mushrooms are golden and crispy.
7. Garnish with fresh parsley and serve hot.

Smoky Chilli Chips with Garlic Dip

SERVES: 4

Ingredients:
4 large potatoes, cut into chips
3 tbsps. olive oil, divided
1 tsp. smoked chilli powder
Salt and freshly ground black pepper
1 whole garlic bulb
100 ml sour cream
1 tbsp. lemon juice
Fresh chives, chopped, for garnish
Cooking spray

PREP TIME: 10 minutes
COOK TIME: 20 minutes

Directions:
1. Preheat the Air fryer to 200°C.
2. Toss the potato chips in 2 tbsps. olive oil, smoked chilli powder, salt, and pepper.
3. Grease the Air fryer basket with cooking spray.
4. Place the chips in the basket and air fry for 20 minutes, shaking halfway through.
5. Meanwhile, cut the top off the garlic bulb, drizzle with the remaining tbsp. olive oil, wrap in foil.
6. After the chips are cooked for 5 minutes, place the foil in the air fryer for 15 minutes until soft.
7. Squeeze the roasted garlic into a bowl, mix with sour cream, lemon juice, salt, and pepper.
8. Serve the chips hot with the garlic dip, garnished with chopped chives.

Crispy Pakora Bites

SERVES: 4

PREP TIME: 15 minutes
COOK TIME: 12 minutes

Ingredients:
200 g chickpea flour
1 tsp. turmeric
1 tsp. ground cumin
1 tsp. ground coriander
1 tsp. chilli powder
1 small onion, finely chopped
2 potatoes, peeled and grated
100 g spinach, chopped
1 green chilli, finely chopped
Salt to taste
Water, as needed
Cooking spray

Directions:
1. In a large bowl, mix the chickpea flour, turmeric, cumin, coriander, chilli powder, and salt.
2. Add the chopped onion, grated potatoes, spinach, and green chilli to the bowl.
3. Gradually add water and mix until you have a thick batter.
4. Preheat the Air fryer to 180°C and grease the Air fryer basket with cooking spray.
5. Drop spoonfuls of the batter into the basket, forming small fritters.
6. Air fry for 12 minutes, flipping halfway through, until golden and crispy.
7. Serve hot with your favourite chutney.

Five-Spice Whitebait

SERVES: 4

PREP TIME: 10 minutes
COOK TIME: 10 minutes

Ingredients:
300 g whitebait
2 tbsps. plain flour
1 tsp. Chinese five-spice powder
Salt and freshly ground black pepper
1 lemon, cut into wedges
Fresh coriander, for garnish
Cooking spray

Directions:
1. Preheat the Air fryer to 190°C.
2. In a bowl, mix the flour, five-spice powder, salt, and pepper.
3. Toss the whitebait in the seasoned flour, shaking off excess.
4. Grease the Air fryer basket with cooking spray.
5. Place the whitebait in the basket and air fry for 10 minutes, shaking halfway through, until crispy and golden.
6. Serve hot with lemon wedges and garnished with fresh coriander.

Cheese and Cranberry Fondue Star

SERVES: 4

Ingredients:
1 sheet puff pastry
150 g Brie or Camembert cheese, cut into small pieces
2 tbsps. cranberry sauce
1 tsp. fresh thyme leaves
1 egg, beaten
Cooking spray

Directions:
1. Preheat the Air fryer to 180°C.
2. Roll out the puff pastry and cut it into star shapes using a star-shaped cutter.
3. Place a small piece of cheese and a dab of cranberry sauce in the centre of each star.
4. Fold the pastry over the filling and pinch the edges to seal.
5. Brush the stars with beaten egg and sprinkle with thyme leaves.
6. Grease the Air fryer basket with cooking spray.
7. Place the pastry stars in the basket and bake for 12 minutes or until golden and puffed.
8. Serve warm as a festive snack or starter.

PREP TIME: 15 minutes
COOK TIME: 12 minutes

Spicy Nut and Seed Mix

SERVES: 4

Ingredients:
200 g mixed nuts (almonds, cashews, walnuts)
50 g mixed seeds (pumpkin, sunflower, sesame)
1 tbsp. soy sauce
1 tbsp. honey
1 tsp. chilli flakes
1 tbsp. olive oil
Cooking spray

Directions:
1. Preheat the Air fryer to 180°C and grease the Air fryer basket with cooking spray.
2. In a bowl, mix the nuts and seeds with soy sauce, honey, chilli flakes, and olive oil until well coated.
3. Spread the nut and seed mixture evenly in the basket.
4. Roast for 10 minutes, shaking halfway through, until golden and crispy.
5. Let cool before serving as a crunchy snack.

PREP TIME: 5 minutes
COOK TIME: 10 minutes

Chapter 6: Snacks and Starters / 39

Smoked Salmon Crostini

SERVES: 4

PREP TIME: 10 minutes
COOK TIME: 10 minutes

Ingredients:
8 slices of baguette
100 g cream cheese
100 g smoked salmon
1 tbsp. capers
1 tbsp. fresh dill, chopped
1 lemon, cut into wedges
Cooking spray

Directions:
1. Preheat the Air fryer to 200°C and grease the Air fryer basket with cooking spray.
2. Place half of the baguette slices in the basket and grill for 5 minutes or until toasted.
3. Repeat with the remaining baguette slices.
4. Spread cream cheese on each toasted baguette slice.
5. Top with smoked salmon, capers, and chopped dill.
6. Serve with lemon wedges.

Bengali Beetroot Croquettes

SERVES: 4

PREP TIME: 20 minutes
COOK TIME: 15 minutes

Ingredients:
3 medium beetroots, cooked and grated
2 potatoes, boiled and mashed
1 small onion, finely chopped
2 green chillies, finely chopped
1 tsp. ground cumin
1 tsp. ground coriander
Salt to taste
120 g breadcrumbs
1 egg, beaten (or flax egg for vegan version)
Cooking spray

Directions:
1. In a large bowl, mix the grated beetroot, mashed potatoes, chopped onion, green chillies, cumin, coriander, and salt.
2. Form the mixture into small croquettes.
3. Dip each croquette in the beaten egg, then coat with breadcrumbs.
4. Preheat the Air fryer to 180°C and grease the Air fryer basket with cooking spray.
5. Place the croquettes in the basket and air fry for 15 minutes, flipping halfway through, until golden and crispy.
6. Serve hot with a cooling raita or dip.

Chapter 6: Snacks and Starters

Camembert Bread Bowl

SERVES: 4

Ingredients:
1 whole Camembert cheese
1 round loaf of bread
2 cloves garlic, thinly sliced
2 sprigs rosemary
1 tbsp. olive oil
Cooking spray

Directions:
1. Preheat the Air fryer to 180°C.
2. Cut the top off the round loaf of bread and hollow out the centre to fit the Camembert.
3. Score the top of the Camembert and insert garlic slices and rosemary sprigs into the cuts.
4. Drizzle with olive oil.
5. Place the Camembert in the hollowed-out bread.
6. Grease the Air fryer basket with cooking spray.
7. Place the bread bowl in the basket and bake for 15 minutes or until the cheese is melted and bubbly.
8. Serve hot, ideal for dipping with the bread pieces.

PREP TIME: 10 minutes
COOK TIME: 15 minutes

Spiced Cauliflower Fritters

SERVES: 4

Ingredients:
1 small cauliflower, grated
1 small onion, finely chopped
2 cloves garlic, minced
1 tsp. ground cumin
1 tsp. ground coriander
1 tsp. chilli powder
2 tbsps. chickpea flour
1 egg, beaten (or flax egg for vegan version)
Salt to taste
Cooking spray

Directions:
1. In a large bowl, mix the grated cauliflower, chopped onion, minced garlic, cumin, coriander, chilli powder, chickpea flour, egg, and salt.
2. Form the mixture into small fritters.
3. Preheat the Air fryer to 180°C and grease the Air fryer basket with cooking spray.
4. Place the fritters in the basket and air fry for 12 minutes, flipping halfway through, until golden and crispy.
5. Serve hot with a yoghurt dip or chutney.

PREP TIME: 15 minutes
COOK TIME: 12 minutes

Paneer and Pepper Skewers with Gooseberry Raita

SERVES: 4

PREP TIME: 15 minutes
COOK TIME: 10 minutes

Ingredients:
- 200 g paneer, cubed
- 1 red pepper, cut into squares
- 1 yellow pepper, cut into squares
- 1 tbsp. olive oil
- 1 tsp. ground cumin
- 1 tsp. ground coriander
- Salt and freshly ground black pepper

For the Gooseberry Raita:
- 100 g gooseberries, halved
- 200 ml plain yoghurt
- 1 tbsp. fresh mint, chopped
- 1 tbsp. honey
- Salt to taste
- Cooking spray
- Wooden or metal skewers

Directions:
1. In a bowl, toss the paneer cubes and pepper squares with olive oil, ground cumin, ground coriander, salt, and pepper.
2. Thread the paneer and peppers onto the skewers alternately.
3. Preheat the Air fryer to 200°C and grease the Air fryer basket with cooking spray.
4. Place the skewers in the basket and grill for 10 minutes, turning halfway through, until the paneer is golden and the peppers are tender.
5. For the gooseberry raita, mix the halved gooseberries, plain yoghurt, fresh mint, honey, and salt in a bowl.
6. Serve the skewers hot with the gooseberry raita.

Chaat Platter

SERVES: 4

PREP TIME: 15 minutes
COOK TIME: 10 minutes

Ingredients:
- 2 large potatoes, diced
- 1 tsp. chaat masala
- 1 tsp. ground cumin
- Salt and freshly ground black pepper
- 200 g chickpeas, drained and rinsed
- 1 tbsp. olive oil
- 1 small red onion, finely chopped
- 2 tomatoes, diced
- 1 cucumber, diced
- Fresh coriander, chopped

For the Toppings:
- Tamarind chutney
- Mint chutney
- Yoghurt
- Sev (crunchy chickpea noodles)
- Pomegranate seeds
- Cooking spray

Directions:
1. In a bowl, toss the diced potatoes with olive oil, chaat masala, ground cumin, salt, and pepper.
2. Preheat the Air fryer to 200°C and grease the Air fryer basket with cooking spray.
3. Place the potatoes in the basket and air fry for 10 minutes, shaking halfway through, until crispy and golden.
4. Mix the air-fried potatoes with chickpeas, red onion, tomatoes, cucumber, and chopped coriander in a large bowl.
5. Serve the mixture topped with tamarind chutney, mint chutney, yoghurt, sev, and pomegranate seeds.

Chapter 6: Snacks and Starters

Chapter 7: Desserts and Sweet Treats

Lemon Meringue Tartlets

SERVES: 6

Ingredients:
1 sheet shortcrust pastry
3 large eggs, separated
200 g caster sugar
2 lemons, zested and juiced
50 g butter, melted
1 tbsp. cornflour
150 ml water
Cooking spray

PREP TIME: 20 minutes
COOK TIME: 15 minutes

Directions:
1. Preheat the Air fryer to 180°C and grease tartlet tins with cooking spray.
2. Roll out the shortcrust pastry and cut circles to fit the tartlet tins.
3. Press the pastry circles into the tins and prick the bases with a fork.
4. Place the tartlet tins in the Air fryer basket and bake for 8 minutes or until lightly golden.
5. In a saucepan, mix the lemon juice, zest, water, cornflour, and 100 g of the caster sugar. Cook over medium heat until thickened.
6. Remove from heat and whisk in the egg yolks and melted butter.
7. Fill the baked tartlet shells with the lemon filling.
8. In a clean bowl, whisk the egg whites until stiff peaks form, then gradually add the remaining caster sugar.
9. Spoon the meringue over the lemon filling, making sure it touches the edges of the pastry.
10. Place the tartlet tins back in the air fryer and bake for an additional 7 minutes, or until the meringue is golden.
11. Allow to cool before serving.

Rhubarb and Custard Brioche Bake

SERVES: 6

Ingredients:
200 g rhubarb, chopped
50 g caster sugar
1 brioche loaf, sliced
250 ml custard
2 eggs
1 tsp. vanilla extract
1 tbsp. demerara sugar
Cooking spray

PREP TIME: 20 minutes
COOK TIME: 25 minutes

Directions:
1. Preheat the Air fryer to 180°C.
2. In a bowl, toss the rhubarb with caster sugar and set aside.
3. Arrange the brioche slices in a greased air fryer-safe baking dish.
4. In another bowl, whisk together the custard, eggs, and vanilla extract.
5. Pour the custard mixture over the brioche slices, ensuring they are well soaked.
6. Scatter the sugared rhubarb over the top and sprinkle with demerara sugar.
7. Place the baking dish in the Air fryer basket and bake for 25 minutes or until the top is golden and the custard is set.
8. Serve warm.

Blueberry Bliss Cheesecake

SERVES: 8

PREP TIME: 15 minutes
COOK TIME: 35 minutes

Ingredients:
200 g blueberries
600 g cream cheese, softened
200 g caster sugar
4 large eggs
250 ml double cream
1 tsp. vanilla extract
2 tbsps. plain flour
Cooking spray

Directions:
1. Preheat the Air fryer to 180°C and grease a springform pan with cooking spray.
2. In a large bowl, beat the cream cheese and sugar until smooth.
3. Add the eggs one at a time, beating well after each addition.
4. Stir in the double cream, vanilla extract, and flour until fully incorporated.
5. Fold in the blueberries gently.
6. Pour the mixture into the prepared springform pan.
7. Place the pan in the Air fryer basket and bake for 35 minutes or until the cheesecake is set and the top is golden.
8. Allow to cool completely before serving.

Pear and Butter Puff Strudel

SERVES: 4

PREP TIME: 20 minutes
COOK TIME: 20 minutes

Ingredients:
3 pears, peeled and thinly sliced
50 g unsalted butter, browned
2 tbsps. brown sugar
1 tsp. ground cinnamon
1 sheet puff pastry
1 egg, beaten
Cooking spray

Directions:
1. Preheat the Air fryer to 180°C and grease the Air fryer basket with cooking spray.
2. In a bowl, toss the sliced pears with browned butter, brown sugar, and ground cinnamon.
3. Roll out the puff pastry on a lightly floured surface.
4. Arrange the pear mixture in the centre of the pastry.
5. Fold the pastry over the pears to enclose them, and seal the edges.
6. Brush the pastry with the beaten egg.
7. Carefully transfer the strudel to the Air fryer basket.
8. Bake for 20 minutes or until the pastry is golden and crisp.
9. Allow to cool slightly before serving.

Apple Hazelnut Galette

SERVES: 6

Ingredients:
1 sheet puff pastry
3 apples, thinly sliced
50 g hazelnuts, chopped
2 tbsps. brown sugar
1 tsp. ground cinnamon
1 tsp. fresh rosemary, chopped
1 egg, beaten
Cooking spray

Directions:
1. Preheat the Air fryer to 180°C and grease the Air fryer basket with cooking spray.
2. Roll out the puff pastry on a lightly floured surface.
3. In a bowl, toss the apple slices with brown sugar, cinnamon, chopped hazelnuts, and fresh rosemary.
4. Arrange the apple mixture in the centre of the puff pastry, leaving a border around the edges.
5. Fold the edges of the pastry over the apples to create a rustic edge.
6. Brush the pastry edges with the beaten egg.
7. Carefully transfer the galette to the Air fryer basket.
8. Bake for 25 minutes or until the pastry is golden and the apples are tender.
9. Allow to cool slightly before serving.

PREP TIME: 15 minutes
COOK TIME: 25 minutes

Black Forest Bakewell Delight

SERVES: 8

Ingredients:
200 g fresh or frozen cherries, pitted
1 ready-made shortcrust pastry
100 g ground almonds
100 g caster sugar
100 g unsalted butter, softened
2 large eggs
1 tsp. almond extract
50 g dark chocolate, grated
50 g flaked almonds
Cooking spray

Directions:
1. Preheat the Air fryer to 180°C and grease a tart tin with cooking spray.
2. Roll out the shortcrust pastry and line the greased tart tin.
3. In a large bowl, cream together the butter and sugar until light and fluffy.
4. Beat in the eggs one at a time, then stir in the almond extract and ground almonds.
5. Spread half of the almond mixture over the pastry base.
6. Scatter the cherries and grated chocolate over the almond mixture.
7. Spread the remaining almond mixture over the top, smoothing it out.
8. Sprinkle the flaked almonds over the top.
9. Place the tart tin in the Air fryer basket and bake for 30 minutes or until the top is golden and set.
10. Allow to cool slightly before serving.

PREP TIME: 25 minutes
COOK TIME: 30 minutes

Chapter 7: Desserts and Sweet Treats / 45

Caramelised White Chocolate Dream Cake

SERVES: 4-6

PREP TIME: 20 minutes
COOK TIME: 30 minutes

Ingredients:
100 g digestive biscuits, crushed
50 g unsalted butter, melted
150 g white chocolate, chopped
300 g cream cheese, softened
75 g caster sugar
2 large eggs
100 ml double cream
½ tsp. vanilla extract
Cooking spray

Directions:
1. Preheat the Air fryer to 160°C and grease a 15-cm springform pan with cooking spray.
2. Mix the crushed biscuits with the melted butter and press into the bottom of the greased pan to form the crust.
3. In a large bowl, beat the cream cheese and sugar until smooth.
4. Add the eggs one at a time, beating well after each addition.
5. Stir in the double cream and vanilla extract until fully incorporated.
6. Melt the white chocolate in a microwave or double boiler and fold into the cream cheese mixture.
7. Pour the mixture over the crust in the springform pan.
8. Place the pan in the Air fryer basket and bake for 30 minutes or until the cheesecake is set and the top is golden.
9. Allow to cool completely before serving.

Japanese Fluffy Cheesecake

SERVES: 8

PREP TIME: 20 minutes
COOK TIME: 40 minutes

Ingredients:
200 g cream cheese, softened
50 g unsalted butter, melted
100 ml milk
4 large eggs, separated
100 g caster sugar
60 g plain flour
20 g cornflour
1 tsp. lemon juice
1 tsp. vanilla extract
Cooking spray

Directions:
1. Preheat the Air fryer to 160°C and grease a springform pan with cooking spray.
2. In a large bowl, mix the cream cheese, melted butter, and milk until smooth.
3. Add the egg yolks, lemon juice, and vanilla extract, and mix until well combined.
4. Sift the flour and cornflour into the mixture and stir until smooth.
5. In another bowl, beat the egg whites until frothy. Gradually add the caster sugar and beat until stiff peaks form.
6. Gently fold the egg whites into the cream cheese mixture until well combined.
7. Pour the batter into the greased springform pan.
8. Place the pan in the Air fryer basket and bake for 40 minutes or until the cheesecake is set and lightly golden.
9. Allow to cool completely before serving.

Chapter 7: Desserts and Sweet Treats

Honeyed Flapjacks

SERVES: 8

Ingredients:
200 g porridge oats
100 g unsalted butter
100 g brown sugar
3 tbsps. honey
1 tsp. vanilla extract
Cooking spray

Directions:
1. Preheat the Air fryer to 180°C and grease an air fryer-safe baking dish with cooking spray.
2. In a saucepan, melt the butter, brown sugar, and honey over medium heat until smooth.
3. Remove from heat and stir in the vanilla extract.
4. In a large bowl, mix the porridge oats with the melted butter mixture until well combined.
5. Press the mixture evenly into the greased baking dish.
6. Place the dish in the Air fryer basket and bake for 15 minutes or until golden.
7. Allow to cool completely before cutting into squares and serving.

PREP TIME: 10 minutes
COOK TIME: 15 minutes

Zesty Lemon Drizzle Cake

SERVES: 8

Ingredients:
200 g self-raising flour
200 g unsalted butter, softened
200 g caster sugar
3 large eggs
1 lemon, zested and juiced
50 g icing sugar
Cooking spray

Directions:
1. Preheat the Air fryer to 180°C and grease a loaf pan with cooking spray.
2. In a large bowl, cream together the butter and caster sugar until light and fluffy.
3. Beat in the eggs one at a time, then stir in the lemon zest and juice.
4. Fold in the self-raising flour until fully combined.
5. Pour the batter into the greased loaf pan.
6. Place the loaf pan in the Air fryer basket and bake for 30 minutes, or until a skewer inserted into the centre comes out clean.
7. In a small bowl, mix the icing sugar with a bit of lemon juice to make a glaze.
8. Once the cake is baked, prick the top with a skewer and pour the lemon glaze over the top while the cake is still warm.
9. Allow to cool completely before slicing and serving.

PREP TIME: 15 minutes
COOK TIME: 30 minutes

Chapter 7: Desserts and Sweet Treats / 47

Blackberry Millefeuille Delight

SERVES: 4

PREP TIME: 20 minutes
COOK TIME: 15 minutes

Ingredients:
1 sheet puff pastry
200 g blackberries
200 ml double cream
2 tbsps. icing sugar
1 tsp. vanilla extract
1 tbsp. caster sugar
Cooking spray

Directions:
1. Preheat the Air fryer to 180°C and grease the Air fryer basket with cooking spray.
2. Roll out the puff pastry and cut it into rectangles.
3. Place the pastry rectangles in the Air fryer basket and bake for 10-12 minutes or until golden and puffed.
4. In a bowl, whip the double cream with the icing sugar and vanilla extract until stiff peaks form.
5. In another bowl, toss the blackberries with caster sugar.
6. Once the pastry rectangles are cooled, assemble the millefeuille by layering pastry, whipped cream, and blackberries, repeating to form multiple layers.
7. Serve immediately, dusted with extra icing sugar if desired.

Honeyed Figs with Sesame Crunch

SERVES: 4

PREP TIME: 15 minutes
COOK TIME: 15 minutes

Ingredients:
8 fresh figs, halved
2 tbsps. honey
200 ml crème fraîche
50 g sesame seeds
100 g caster sugar
1 tbsp. water
Cooking spray

Directions:
1. Preheat the Air fryer to 180°C and grease a small baking tray with cooking spray.
2. In a saucepan, combine the caster sugar and water. Cook on low heat for 10 minutes, or until the sugar dissolves and turns a golden caramel colour.
3. Stir in the sesame seeds and pour the mixture onto the greased baking tray. Allow to cool and harden.
4. Break the sesame brittle into pieces.
5. Place the fig halves in the Air fryer basket, drizzle with honey, and bake for 5 minutes until warm.
6. Serve the warm figs with a dollop of crème fraîche and pieces of sesame brittle.

Classic Lemon Tart

SERVES: 8

Ingredients:
1 sheet shortcrust pastry
4 large eggs
200 ml double cream
200 g caster sugar
3 lemons, zested and juiced
Cooking spray

Directions:
1. Preheat the Air fryer to 180°C and grease a tart tin with cooking spray.
2. Roll out the shortcrust pastry and line the greased tart tin.
3. In a large bowl, whisk together the eggs, double cream, caster sugar, lemon zest, and lemon juice until smooth.
4. Pour the mixture into the pastry-lined tart tin.
5. Place the tart tin in the Air fryer basket and bake for 25 minutes or until the filling is set and lightly golden.
6. Allow to cool before serving.

PREP TIME: 20 minutes
COOK TIME: 25 minutes

Apple Crumble Cupcakes

SERVES: 12

Ingredients:
200 g self-raising flour
200 g unsalted butter, softened
200 g caster sugar
3 large eggs
2 apples, peeled, cored, and diced
1 tsp. ground cinnamon

For the Crumble Topping:
50 g plain flour
50 g demerara sugar
25 g unsalted butter, cubed
Cooking spray

Directions:
1. Preheat the Air fryer to 180°C and grease a 12-cup muffin tin with cooking spray.
2. In a large bowl, cream together the butter and caster sugar until light and fluffy.
3. Beat in the eggs one at a time until fully combined.
4. Fold in the self-raising flour, ground cinnamon, and diced apples.
5. Divide the batter evenly among the muffin cases.
6. In a separate bowl, mix the plain flour, demerara sugar, and cubed butter with your fingers until it resembles breadcrumbs.
7. Sprinkle the crumble topping over the batter in each muffin case.
8. Place the 6 muffin cases in the Air fryer basket and bake for 15 minutes or until a skewer inserted into the centre comes out clean.
9. Repeat with the remaining muffin cases.
10. Allow to cool slightly before serving.

PREP TIME: 20 minutes
COOK TIME: 30 minutes

Chapter 7: Desserts and Sweet Treats / 49

Chapter 8: Holiday and Party Dishes

Chocolate Yule Log

SERVES: 8

PREP TIME: 30 minutes
COOK TIME: 12 minutes

Ingredients:
4 large eggs, separated
100 g caster sugar
50 g plain flour
25 g cocoa powder

For the Filling and Topping:
200 ml double cream
100 g dark chocolate, melted
Icing sugar, for dusting

Directions:
1. Preheat the Air fryer to 180°C and line a Swiss roll tin with parchment paper.
2. In a large bowl, whisk the egg yolks with the caster sugar until thick and pale.
3. Sift the flour and cocoa powder into the egg yolk mixture and fold gently to combine.
4. In a separate bowl, whisk the egg whites until stiff peaks form. Fold the egg whites into the chocolate mixture.
5. Spread the mixture evenly in the prepared Swiss roll tin.
6. Place the tin in the Air fryer basket and bake for 12 minutes, or until the sponge is springy to the touch.
7. Turn the sponge out onto a sheet of parchment paper dusted with icing sugar and roll up from the short end. Allow to cool.
8. Whip the double cream until soft peaks form and fold in the melted dark chocolate.
9. Unroll the sponge, spread with the chocolate cream, and re-roll. Dust with icing sugar before serving.

Bacon-Wrapped Roast Turkey

SERVES: 8

PREP TIME: 20 minutes
COOK TIME: 60 minutes

Ingredients:
1 turkey breast (approximately 1.5 kg)
8-10 rashers of streaky bacon
2 tbsps. olive oil
1 tbsp. fresh thyme, chopped
1 tbsp. fresh rosemary, chopped
Salt and freshly ground black pepper
Cooking spray

Directions:
1. Preheat the Air fryer to 180°C and grease the Air fryer basket with cooking spray.
2. In a small bowl, mix the olive oil, thyme, rosemary, salt, and pepper.
3. Rub the turkey breast with the herb mixture.
4. Lay the streaky bacon rashers over the turkey breast to form a lattice pattern.
5. Place the turkey breast in the Air fryer basket.
6. Roast for 60 minutes, or until the internal temperature reaches 75°C. Check the turkey breast at the 40-minute mark and cover with foil if the bacon starts to brown too quickly.
7. Allow to rest for 10 minutes before slicing and serving.

50 \ Chapter 8: Holiday and Party Dishes

Hasselback Swede Gratin

SERVES: 4

Ingredients:
1 large swede, peeled and thinly sliced
100 ml double cream
100 g grated Parmesan cheese
2 cloves garlic, minced
1 tbsp. fresh thyme, chopped
Salt and freshly ground black pepper
Cooking spray

PREP TIME: 15 minutes
COOK TIME: 40 minutes

Directions:
1. Preheat the Air fryer to 180°C and grease a small baking dish with cooking spray.
2. Arrange the thinly sliced swede in the baking dish in a fan pattern.
3. In a bowl, mix the double cream, minced garlic, chopped thyme, salt, and pepper.
4. Pour the cream mixture over the swede slices.
5. Sprinkle the grated Parmesan cheese over the top.
6. Place the dish in the Air fryer basket.
7. Bake for 40 minutes, or until the swede is tender and the top is golden and bubbly.
8. Allow to cool slightly before serving.

Cheese Mustard Straws

SERVES: 4

Ingredients:
1 sheet puff pastry
100 g mature cheddar cheese, grated
1 tbsp. Dijon mustard
1 egg, beaten
1 tsp. paprika
Salt and freshly ground black pepper
Cooking spray

PREP TIME: 15 minutes
COOK TIME: 12 minutes per batch

Directions:
1. Preheat the Air fryer to 180°C and grease the Air fryer basket with cooking spray.
2. Roll out the puff pastry on a lightly floured surface.
3. Spread the Dijon mustard evenly over the pastry.
4. Sprinkle the grated cheddar cheese, paprika, salt, and pepper over the mustard.
5. Fold the pastry in half and roll out again to flatten.
6. Cut the pastry into thin strips and twist each strip several times.
7. Place 4-5 strips in the Air fryer basket, ensuring they are not touching. Cook in batches if necessary.
8. Brush the strips with beaten egg.
9. Bake for 12 minutes, or until golden and crispy.
10. Allow to cool slightly before serving.

Chapter 8: Holiday and Party Dishes / 51

Turkey Koftas with Cranberry Dip

SERVES: 4

PREP TIME: 20 minutes
COOK TIME: 15 minutes per batch

Ingredients:
500 g minced turkey
1 small onion, grated
2 cloves garlic, minced
1 tsp. ground cumin
1 tsp. ground coriander
1 tsp. paprika
1 egg, beaten
Salt and freshly ground black pepper
Fresh parsley, chopped, for garnish

For the Dip:
100 g cranberry sauce
2 tbsps. tahini
1 tbsp. lemon juice
Salt and freshly ground black pepper
Cooking spray

Directions:
1. Preheat the Air fryer to 180°C and grease the Air fryer basket with cooking spray.
2. In a large bowl, mix the minced turkey, grated onion, minced garlic, ground cumin, ground coriander, paprika, beaten egg, salt, and pepper.
3. Shape the mixture into small koftas (about 8-10).
4. Place 4-5 koftas in the Air fryer basket, ensuring they are not touching. Cook in batches if necessary.
5. Air fry for 15 minutes, or until golden and cooked through, turning halfway through.
6. For the dip, mix the cranberry sauce, tahini, lemon juice, salt, and pepper in a bowl until well combined.
7. Serve the koftas with the cranberry dip and garnish with chopped parsley.

Cheesy Salmon Wreath

SERVES: 6

PREP TIME: 20 minutes
COOK TIME: 15 minutes

Ingredients:
100 g plain flour
75 g unsalted butter
3 large eggs
100 g grated cheddar cheese
100 g hot smoked salmon, flaked
1 tbsp. horseradish sauce
100 ml crème fraîche
Fresh dill, chopped
Salt and freshly ground black pepper
Cooking spray

Directions:
1. Preheat the Air fryer to 200°C and grease the Air fryer basket with cooking spray.
2. In a saucepan, heat 150 ml of water and the butter until it boils. Remove from heat and quickly stir in the flour.
3. Return to heat and cook, stirring constantly, until the mixture forms a ball and leaves the sides of the pan.
4. Cool slightly, then beat in the eggs one at a time until smooth. Stir in the grated cheese and season with salt and pepper.
5. Spoon the choux pastry into a piping bag and pipe small mounds into a wreath shape in the Air fryer basket.
6. Bake for 15 minutes, or until puffed and golden.
7. Mix the hot smoked salmon with the horseradish sauce and crème fraîche. Season with salt, pepper, and chopped dill.
8. Serve the choux wreath with the salmon dip.

Game Terrine with Brandy Prunes

SERVES: 4

Ingredients:
- 200 g pork belly, minced
- 200 g venison, minced
- 100 g chicken livers, chopped
- 50 g breadcrumbs
- 2 tbsps. brandy
- 100 g prunes, chopped and soaked in brandy for at least an hour
- 1 small onion, finely chopped
- 2 cloves garlic, minced
- 1 tsp. dried thyme
- 1 tsp. dried sage
- 2 large eggs, beaten
- Salt and freshly ground black pepper
- Cooking spray

PREP TIME: 20 minutes (plus 1 hour soaking time)
COOK TIME: 1 hour

Directions:
1. Preheat the Air fryer to 160°C and grease a terrine mould or loaf tin with cooking spray.
2. In a large bowl, mix the minced pork belly, venison, and chopped chicken livers with the breadcrumbs, brandy, soaked prunes, chopped onion, minced garlic, dried thyme, dried sage, and beaten eggs. Season with salt and pepper.
3. Spoon the mixture into the prepared mould or tin, pressing down firmly.
4. Cover with foil.
5. Place the mould or tin in the Air fryer basket and bake for 1 hour, or until the terrine is set and cooked through.
6. Allow to cool completely before turning out and slicing to serve.

Creamy Bacon Sprouts

SERVES: 4

Ingredients:
- 500 g Brussels sprouts, trimmed and halved
- 100 g bacon, chopped
- 100 g cooked chestnuts, chopped
- 200 ml double cream
- 1 tbsp. olive oil
- Salt and freshly ground black pepper
- Cooking spray

PREP TIME: 15 minutes
COOK TIME: 20 minutes

Directions:
1. Preheat the Air fryer to 180°C and grease the Air fryer basket with cooking spray.
2. In a large bowl, toss the Brussels sprouts with olive oil, salt, and pepper.
3. Place the sprouts in the Air fryer basket and roast for 15 minutes, shaking halfway through.
4. Add the chopped bacon and chestnuts to the basket and roast for an additional 5 minutes.
5. Remove the sprouts, bacon, and chestnuts from the air fryer and transfer to a serving dish.
6. Pour the double cream over the mixture, stirring to combine.
7. Serve immediately.

Chapter 8: Holiday and Party Dishes / 53

Walnut Cheese Rolls

SERVES: 4

PREP TIME: 15 minutes
COOK TIME: 15 minutes per batch

Ingredients:
200 g mature cheddar cheese, grated
50 g pickled walnuts, chopped
1 sheet puff pastry
1 egg, beaten
1 tsp. Dijon mustard
Fresh parsley, chopped, for garnish
Salt and freshly ground black pepper
Cooking spray

Directions:
1. Preheat the Air fryer to 180°C and grease the Air fryer basket with cooking spray.
2. In a bowl, mix the grated cheddar cheese, chopped pickled walnuts, Dijon mustard, salt, and pepper.
3. Roll out the puff pastry on a lightly floured surface.
4. Spread the cheese mixture over the pastry, leaving a small border.
5. Roll up the pastry tightly and slice into individual rolls.
6. Brush the rolls with beaten egg.
7. Place 2-3 rolls in the Air fryer basket, ensuring they are not touching. Cook in batches if necessary.
8. Bake for 15 minutes, or until the pastry is golden and the cheese is melted and bubbly.
9. Garnish with chopped parsley before serving.

Halloumi Clementine Salad

SERVES: 4

PREP TIME: 15 minutes
COOK TIME: 10 minutes

Ingredients:
200 g halloumi, sliced
2 clementines, peeled and segmented
150 g cooked pearl barley
1 bag mixed salad leaves
2 tbsps. olive oil
1 tbsp. lemon juice
1 tsp. honey
Salt and freshly ground black pepper
Fresh mint leaves, chopped, for garnish
Cooking spray

Directions:
1. Preheat the Air fryer to 200°C and grease the Air fryer basket with cooking spray.
2. Brush the halloumi slices with a little olive oil.
3. Place the halloumi slices in the Air fryer basket and grill for 10 minutes, turning halfway through, until golden and crispy.
4. In a large bowl, mix the cooked pearl barley, clementine segments, and mixed salad leaves.
5. In a small bowl, whisk together the remaining olive oil, lemon juice, honey, salt, and pepper.
6. Pour the dressing over the salad and toss to combine.
7. Top the salad with the grilled halloumi and garnish with chopped mint leaves before serving.

Crab Croquettes with Romesco Sauce

SERVES: 4

Ingredients:
200 g cooked crab meat
1 small onion, finely chopped
1 clove garlic, minced
1 tbsp. butter
2 tbsps. plain flour
150 ml milk
1 egg, beaten
100 g breadcrumbs
Salt and freshly ground black pepper

For the Romesco Sauce:
1 red pepper, roasted and peeled
50 g blanched almonds
1 clove garlic
1 tbsp. red wine vinegar
50 ml olive oil
Salt and freshly ground black pepper
Cooking spray

PREP TIME: 20 minutes
COOK TIME: 15 minutes per batch

Directions:
1. In a saucepan over medium heat, melt the butter and sauté the onion and garlic until softened. Stir in the flour and cook for 1 minute.
2. Gradually add the milk, stirring continuously until the mixture thickens. Remove from heat and stir in the crab meat. Season with salt and pepper.
3. Let the mixture cool, then shape into small croquettes.
4. Dip each croquette in beaten egg, then coat with breadcrumbs.
5. Preheat the Air fryer to 180°C and grease the Air fryer basket with cooking spray.
6. Place 6-8 croquettes in the Air fryer basket, ensuring they are not touching. Cook in batches if necessary.
7. Air fry for 15 minutes, or until golden and crispy, shaking halfway through.
8. For the Romesco sauce, blend the roasted red pepper, almonds, garlic, red wine vinegar, and olive oil until smooth. Season with salt and pepper.
9. Serve the croquettes with the Romesco dipping sauce.

Lemon Sage Potatoes Anna

SERVES: 4

Ingredients:
500 g potatoes, thinly sliced
50 g unsalted butter, melted
Zest of 1 lemon
1 tbsp. fresh sage, chopped
Salt and freshly ground black pepper
Cooking spray

PREP TIME: 15 minutes
COOK TIME: 30 minutes

Directions:
1. Preheat the Air fryer to 180°C and grease a small baking dish with cooking spray.
2. In a large bowl, toss the thinly sliced potatoes with melted butter, lemon zest, chopped sage, salt, and pepper.
3. Layer the potatoes in the greased baking dish, pressing down firmly.
4. Place the dish in the Air fryer basket.
5. Bake for 30 minutes, or until the potatoes are tender and the top is golden and crispy.
6. Allow to cool slightly before serving.

Chapter 8: Holiday and Party Dishes

Festive Fruit Cake

SERVES: 6-8

PREP TIME: 30 minutes
COOK TIME: 1 hour to 1 hour 15 minutes

Ingredients:
110 g plain flour
¼ tsp. ground mixed spice
110 g unsalted butter, softened
110 g dark brown sugar
2 large eggs
½ tbsp. black treacle
100 g currants
100 g sultanas
100 g raisins
50 g chopped glacé cherries
50 g mixed peel
Zest of ½ lemon
Zest of ½ orange
25 g almonds, chopped
1½ tbsps. brandy
Cooking spray

Directions:
1. Preheat the Air fryer to 160°C and grease a deep cake tin with cooking spray.
2. In a large bowl, mix the flour and ground mixed spice.
3. In another bowl, cream the butter and dark brown sugar until light and fluffy.
4. Beat in the eggs one at a time, then stir in the black treacle.
5. Fold in the flour mixture, then add the currants, sultanas, raisins, chopped glacé cherries, mixed peel, lemon zest, orange zest, and chopped almonds.
6. Spoon the mixture into the greased cake tin and level the top.
7. Place the tin in the Air fryer basket and bake for 1 hour to 1 hour 15 minutes, or until a skewer inserted into the centre comes out clean.
8. Allow to cool in the tin, then remove and brush with brandy before serving.

Creamy Baked Leeks

SERVES: 4

PREP TIME: 10 minutes
COOK TIME: 20 minutes

Ingredients:
4 large leeks, trimmed and cut into chunks
100 ml double cream
50 g grated Gruyère cheese
2 tbsps. unsalted butter
1 clove garlic, minced
1 tbsp. fresh parsley, chopped
Salt and freshly ground black pepper
Cooking spray

Directions:
1. Preheat the Air fryer to 180°C and grease a small baking dish with cooking spray.
2. In a saucepan over medium-low heat, melt the butter and sauté the garlic until fragrant.
3. Add the leeks and cook for 5 minutes until softened.
4. Transfer the leeks to the greased baking dish.
5. Pour the double cream over the leeks and sprinkle with grated Gruyère cheese.
6. Place the dish in the Air fryer basket.
7. Bake for 20 minutes, or until the leeks are tender and the top is golden and bubbly.
8. Garnish with chopped parsley before serving.

Chapter 9: Family Favourites

Chicken and Mushroom Mini Pies

SERVES: 2

Ingredients:
100 g chicken breast, diced
75 g mushrooms, sliced
1 small onion, chopped
1 clove garlic, minced
100 ml chicken stock
50 ml double cream
½ tbsp. plain flour
½ tsp. dried thyme
Salt and freshly ground black pepper
½ sheet puff pastry
1 egg, beaten
Cooking spray

PREP TIME: 20 minutes
COOK TIME: 21 minutes

Directions:
1. Preheat the Air fryer to 180°C and grease two small pie tins with cooking spray.
2. In a frying pan over medium heat, sauté the onion and garlic until softened. Add the diced chicken and cook until browned.
3. Add the mushrooms and cook for another 5 minutes.
4. Stir in the flour and cook for 1 minute, then gradually add the chicken stock, stirring continuously.
5. Add the double cream and thyme, and simmer until the sauce thickens. Season with salt and pepper.
6. Divide the mixture between the two greased pie tins.
7. Roll out the puff pastry and cut out two circles slightly larger than the pie tins. Place a pastry circle over each pie tin and press the edges to seal.
8. Brush the pastry tops with beaten egg.
9. Place the two pie tins in the Air fryer basket.
10. Bake for 15 minutes or until the pastry is golden and puffed.
11. Allow to cool slightly before serving.

Favourite Sausage Roll Wreath

SERVES: 4-6

Ingredients:
500 g sausage meat
1 small onion, finely chopped
1 clove garlic, minced
1 tsp. dried sage
2 sheets puff pastry
1 egg, beaten
Salt and freshly ground black pepper
Fresh rosemary sprigs, for garnish
Cooking spray

PREP TIME: 20 minutes
COOK TIME: 25 minutes

Directions:
1. Preheat the Air fryer to 180°C and grease the Air fryer basket with cooking spray.
2. In a bowl, mix the sausage meat with the chopped onion, minced garlic, dried sage, salt, and pepper.
3. Roll out the puff pastry sheets on a lightly floured surface.
4. Place the sausage mixture in a line down the centre of each pastry sheet.
5. Fold the pastry over the sausage mixture and press the edges to seal. Cut into small rolls.
6. Arrange the rolls in a wreath shape in the Air fryer basket, ensuring they are touching slightly.
7. Brush the rolls with beaten egg.
8. Bake for 25 minutes or until the pastry is golden and the sausage meat is cooked through.
9. Garnish with fresh rosemary sprigs before serving.

Peppered Steak and Radish Salad

SERVES: 2

PREP TIME: 15 minutes
COOK TIME: 12 minutes

Ingredients:
2 steaks (sirloin or rib-eye)
1 tbsp. olive oil
1 tsp. black pepper, coarsely ground
1 bunch radishes, halved
1 bag mixed salad leaves
1 tbsp. balsamic vinegar
Salt to taste
Cooking spray

Directions:
1. Preheat the Air fryer to 200°C and grease the Air fryer basket with cooking spray.
2. Rub the steaks with olive oil and coat with coarsely ground black pepper and salt.
3. Place the steaks in the Air fryer basket and grill for 4 minutes on each side, or until cooked to your desired level of doneness.
4. Remove the steaks from the air fryer and let them rest.
5. Toss the radishes with a bit of olive oil and place them in the Air fryer basket. Grill for 4 minutes or until slightly charred.
6. In a bowl, combine the salad leaves, grilled radishes, and balsamic vinegar.
7. Slice the steak and serve over the salad.

Smoked Mackerel Melts

SERVES: 4

PREP TIME: 10 minutes
COOK TIME: 8 minutes

Ingredients:
200 g smoked mackerel, flaked
4 slices of crusty bread
100 g cream cheese
1 tbsp. horseradish sauce
1 small red onion, thinly sliced
50 g grated cheddar cheese
Fresh chives, chopped, for garnish
Cooking spray

Directions:
1. Preheat the Air fryer to 200°C and grease the Air fryer basket with cooking spray.
2. In a bowl, mix the cream cheese with the horseradish sauce.
3. Spread the cream cheese mixture on each slice of bread.
4. Top with flaked mackerel, sliced red onion, and grated cheddar cheese.
5. Place the open-faced sandwiches in the Air fryer basket and grill for 8 minutes or until the cheese is melted and bubbly.
6. Garnish with chopped chives before serving.

Eton Mess Roll

SERVES: 6

Ingredients:
4 large eggs, separated
100 g caster sugar
1 tsp. vanilla extract
200 ml double cream
50 g icing sugar
200 g strawberries, hulled and sliced
2 tbsps. strawberry jam
Cooking spray

PREP TIME: 20 minutes
COOK TIME: 10 minutes

Directions:
1. Preheat the Air fryer to 180°C and line a baking tray with parchment paper, then grease it with cooking spray.
2. In a large bowl, whisk the egg yolks and caster sugar until thick and pale. Add the vanilla extract.
3. In another bowl, whisk the egg whites until stiff peaks form. Fold the egg whites into the yolk mixture.
4. Spread the mixture evenly on the prepared baking tray.
5. Place the tray in the Air fryer basket and bake for 10 minutes or until the sponge is golden and springs back when touched.
6. While the sponge cools, whip the double cream with the icing sugar until soft peaks form.
7. Spread the strawberry jam over the cooled sponge, followed by the whipped cream and sliced strawberries.
8. Carefully roll up the sponge from one short end to the other.
9. Slice and serve.

Lemon Curd Cake

SERVES: 6

Ingredients:
200 g self-raising flour
200 g unsalted butter, softened
200 g caster sugar
3 large eggs
1 lemon, zested and juiced
100 g lemon curd
Cooking spray

PREP TIME: 15 minutes
COOK TIME: 25 minutes

Directions:
1. Preheat the Air fryer to 160°C and grease a small cake tin with cooking spray.
2. In a large bowl, cream together the butter and caster sugar until light and fluffy.
3. Beat in the eggs one at a time, then stir in the lemon zest and juice.
4. Fold in the self-raising flour until fully combined.
5. Pour half of the batter into the greased cake tin.
6. Spoon the lemon curd over the batter, then cover with the remaining batter.
7. Place the cake tin in the Air fryer basket and bake for 25 minutes, or until a skewer inserted into the centre comes out clean.
8. Allow to cool slightly before serving.

Chapter 9: Family Favourites / 59

Garlic Butter Chicken Kiev

SERVES: 4

PREP TIME: 15 minutes
COOK TIME: 20 minutes

Ingredients:
4 chicken breasts
100 g unsalted butter, softened
2 cloves garlic, minced
2 tbsps. fresh parsley, chopped
100 g plain flour
2 eggs, beaten
150 g breadcrumbs
Salt and freshly ground black pepper
Cooking spray

Directions:
1. Preheat the Air fryer to 180°C and grease the Air fryer basket with cooking spray.
2. In a small bowl, mix the softened butter, minced garlic, and chopped parsley. Shape into a log, wrap in cling film, and freeze until firm.
3. Using a sharp knife, cut a pocket into the side of each chicken breast.
4. Insert a piece of the garlic butter log into each pocket and secure with toothpicks.
5. Season the flour with salt and pepper. Coat each chicken breast in flour, then dip in beaten eggs, and finally coat with breadcrumbs.
6. Place the chicken breasts in the Air fryer basket, ensuring they are not touching. Cook in batches if necessary.
7. Air fry for 20 minutes, flipping halfway through, until golden and cooked through.
8. Allow to rest for a few minutes before serving.

Homemade English Muffins

SERVES: 8

PREP TIME: 20 minutes, plus 1 hour rising time
COOK TIME: 12 minutes

Ingredients:
450 g strong white bread flour
7 g sachet fast-action yeast
1 tsp. salt
1 tsp. sugar
300 ml warm milk
50 g unsalted butter, melted
Cooking spray

Directions:
1. In a large bowl, mix the flour, yeast, salt, and sugar.
2. Add the warm milk and melted butter, and mix to form a dough.
3. Knead the dough on a floured surface for 5-10 minutes until smooth and elastic.
4. Place the dough in a greased bowl, cover, and let it rise for 1 hour or until doubled in size.
5. Preheat the Air fryer to 180°C and grease the Air fryer basket with cooking spray.
6. Roll out the dough to about 1 cm thickness and cut out rounds using a cookie cutter.
7. Place a few rounds in the Air fryer basket, ensuring they are not touching. Cook in batches if necessary.
8. Bake for 12 minutes or until the muffins are golden and cooked through, flipping halfway through.
9. Allow to cool slightly before serving. Split and toast if desired.

Savoury Sausage Rolls

SERVES: 4

Ingredients:
400 g sausage meat
1 small onion, finely chopped
1 clove garlic, minced
1 tsp. dried sage
Salt and freshly ground black pepper
1 sheet puff pastry
1 egg, beaten
Cooking spray

PREP TIME: 15 minutes
COOK TIME: 15 minutes

Directions:
1. Preheat the Air fryer to 180°C and grease the Air fryer basket with cooking spray.
2. In a bowl, mix the sausage meat with the chopped onion, garlic, sage, salt, and pepper.
3. Roll out the puff pastry on a lightly floured surface.
4. Place the sausage mixture in a line down the centre of the pastry.
5. Fold the pastry over the sausage mixture and press the edges to seal. Cut into individual rolls.
6. Brush the rolls with beaten egg.
7. Place the sausage rolls in the Air fryer basket and bake for 15 minutes or until the pastry is golden and the sausage meat is cooked through.
8. Allow to cool slightly before serving.

Rosemary and Sea Salt Flatbread

SERVES: 4

Ingredients:
250 g strong white bread flour
7 g sachet fast-action yeast
1 tsp. sea salt
150 ml warm water
2 tbsps. olive oil, plus extra for drizzling
1 tbsp. fresh rosemary, chopped
Cooking spray

PREP TIME: 15 minutes, plus 1 hour rising time
COOK TIME: 20 minutes

Directions:
1. In a large bowl, mix the flour, yeast, and sea salt.
2. Make a well in the centre and add the warm water and 1 tbsp. olive oil. Mix to form a dough.
3. Knead the dough on a floured surface for 5-10 minutes until smooth and elastic.
4. Place the dough in a greased bowl, cover, and let it rise for 1 hour or until doubled in size.
5. Preheat the Air fryer to 180°C and grease the Air fryer basket with cooking spray.
6. Roll out the dough to fit the Air fryer basket.
7. Press the dough into the basket and drizzle with olive oil. Sprinkle with chopped rosemary and sea salt.
8. Bake for 20 minutes or until golden and cooked through.
9. Allow to cool slightly before serving.

Chapter 9: Family Favourites / 61

Herb-Crusted Roast Beef

SERVES: 4

PREP TIME: 15 minutes
COOK TIME: 45 minutes

Ingredients:
1 kg topside of beef
2 tbsps. olive oil
2 cloves garlic, minced
2 tbsps. fresh rosemary, chopped
2 tbsps. fresh thyme, chopped
Salt and freshly ground black pepper
Cooking spray

Directions:
1. Preheat the Air fryer to 180°C and grease the Air fryer basket with cooking spray.
2. In a bowl, mix the olive oil, minced garlic, chopped rosemary, chopped thyme, salt, and pepper.
3. Rub the herb mixture all over the topside of beef.
4. Place the beef in the Air fryer basket.
5. Roast for 45 minutes, or until the beef reaches your desired level of doneness (internal temperature should be 60°C for medium-rare).
6. Allow the beef to rest for 10 minutes before slicing and serving.

Lemon Herb Roast Chicken

SERVES: 4

PREP TIME: 20 minutes
COOK TIME: 50 minutes

Ingredients:
1 whole chicken (about 1.5 kg)
1 lemon, halved
2 tbsps. olive oil
2 tsps. dried oregano
Salt and freshly ground black pepper
For the Stuffing:
100 g breadcrumbs
1 clove garlic, minced
1 small onion, finely chopped
1 tbsp. fresh parsley, chopped
1 tbsp. olive oil
Salt and freshly ground black pepper
Cooking spray

Directions:
1. Preheat the Air fryer to 180°C and grease the Air fryer basket with cooking spray.
2. In a bowl, mix the breadcrumbs, minced garlic, chopped onion, fresh parsley, 1 tbsp. olive oil, salt, and pepper to make the stuffing.
3. Stuff the cavity of the chicken with the breadcrumb mixture.
4. Rub the chicken with olive oil, and sprinkle with dried oregano, salt, and pepper. Place the lemon halves inside the cavity.
5. Place the chicken in the Air fryer basket, breast side up.
6. Roast for 50 minutes, or until the chicken is cooked through and the skin is golden brown, flipping halfway through.
7. Allow to rest for 10 minutes before carving and serving.

Chapter 9: Family Favourites

Banana Hot Cross Bread

SERVES: 8

Ingredients:
Cooking spray
3 ripe bananas, mashed
100 g unsalted butter, melted
150 g caster sugar
1 large egg
1 tsp. vanilla extract
1 tsp. ground cinnamon
1 tsp. ground nutmeg
200 g self-raising flour
50 g sultanas
50 g mixed peel
For the Cross:
50 g plain flour
50 ml water

PREP TIME: 15 minutes
COOK TIME: 30 minutes

Directions:
1. Preheat the Air fryer to 160°C and grease a loaf pan with cooking spray.
2. In a large bowl, mix the mashed bananas, melted butter, caster sugar, egg, and vanilla extract until well combined.
3. Stir in the ground cinnamon, ground nutmeg, and self-raising flour until fully incorporated.
4. Fold in the sultanas and mixed peel.
5. Pour the batter into the greased loaf pan.
6. Mix the plain flour with water to form a thick paste and pipe a cross over the top of the batter.
7. Place the loaf pan in the Air fryer basket and bake for 30 minutes, or until a skewer inserted into the centre comes out clean.
8. Allow to cool slightly before slicing and serving.

Salmon Terrine Delight

SERVES: 4

Ingredients:
200 g smoked salmon
200 g fresh salmon, skinned and boned
100 ml double cream
2 tbsps. fresh dill, chopped
1 lemon, zested and juiced
Salt and freshly ground black pepper
Cooking spray

PREP TIME: 20 minutes
COOK TIME: 25 minutes

Directions:
1. Preheat the Air fryer to 180°C and grease a small loaf tin with cooking spray.
2. Line the loaf tin with the smoked salmon slices, ensuring they overlap and hang over the edges.
3. In a food processor, blend the fresh salmon with the double cream, lemon zest, lemon juice, dill, salt, and pepper until smooth.
4. Spoon the salmon mixture into the prepared tin and fold the overhanging smoked salmon slices over the top.
5. Cover the loaf tin with foil.
6. Place the tin in the Air fryer basket and bake for 25 minutes or until the terrine is set and cooked through.
7. Allow to cool completely before turning out and slicing to serve.

Appendix 1: Measurement Conversion Chart

WEIGHT EQUIVALENTS

METRIC	US STANDARD	US STANDARD (OUNCES)
15 g	1 tablespoon	1/2 ounce
30 g	1/8 cup	1 ounce
60 g	1/4 cup	2 ounces
115 g	1/2 cup	4 ounces
170 g	3/4 cup	6 ounces
225 g	1 cup	8 ounces
450 g	2 cups	16 ounces
900 g	4 cups	2 pounds

VOLUME EQUIVALENTS

METRIC	US STANDARD	US STANDARD (OUNCES)
15 ml	1 tablespoon	1/2 fl.oz.
30 ml	2 tablespoons	1 fl.oz.
60 ml	1/4 cup	2 fl.oz.
125 ml	1/2 cup	4 fl.oz.
180 ml	3/4 cup	6 fl.oz.
250 ml	1 cup	8 fl.oz.
500 ml	2 cups	16 fl.oz.
1000 ml	4 cups	1 quart

TEMPERATURES EQUIVALENTS

CELSIUS (C)	FAHRENHEIT (F) (APPROXIMATE)
120 °C	250 °F
135 °C	275 °F
150 °C	300 °F
160 °C	325 °F
175 °C	350 °F
190 °C	375 °F
205 °C	400 °F
220 °C	425 °F
230 °C	450 °F
245°C	475 °F
260 °C	500 °F

LENGTH EQUIVALENTS

METRIC	IMPERIAL
3 mm	1/8 inch
6 mm	1/4 inch
1 cm	1/2 inch
2.5 cm	1 inch
3 cm	1 1/4 inches
5 cm	2 inches
10 cm	4 inches
15 cm	6 inches
20 cm	8 inches

Appendix 2: Air Fryer Cooking Chart

\multicolumn{6}{c}{Vegetable}					
Item	Temp (°C)	Time (mins)	Item	Temp (°C)	Time (mins)
Asparagus (sliced 2-cm)	200°C	5	Mushrooms (sliced ½-cm)	200°C	5
Aubergine (4-cm cubes)	200°C	15	Onions (pearl)	200°C	10
Beetroots (whole)	200°C	40	Parsnips (1-cm chunks)	190°C	15
Broccoli (florets)	200°C	6	Peppers (2-cm chunks)	200°C	15
Brussels Sprouts (halved)	190°C	15	Potatoes (small baby, 650 g)	200°C	14
Carrots (sliced 1-cm)	190°C	15	Potatoes (2-cm chunks)	200°C	15
Cauliflower (florets)	200°C	12	Potatoes (baked whole)	200°C	45
Corn on the cob	200°C	6	Runner Beans	200°C	5
Courgette (1-cm sticks)	200°C	12	Sweet Potato (baked)	190°C	30 to 35
Fennel (quartered)	190°C	15	Tomatoes (cherry)	200°C	4
Kale leaves	120°C	10	Tomatoes (halves)	180°C	10

\multicolumn{6}{c}{Chicken}					
Item	Temp (°C)	Time (mins)	Item	Temp (°C)	Time (mins)
Breasts, bone in (550 g)	190°C	24	Legs, bone in (800 g)	190°C	30
Breasts, boneless (150 g)	190°C	14	Wings (900 g)	200°C	25
Drumsticks (1.1 kg)	190°C	20	Game Hen (halved – 900 g)	200°C	20
Thighs, bone in (900 g)	190°C	22	Whole Chicken (3 kg)	180°C	75
Thighs, boneless (700 g)	190°C	20	Tenders	180°C	8 to 10

\multicolumn{6}{c}{Beef}					
Item	Temp (°C)	Time (mins)	Item	Temp (°C)	Time (mins)
Burger (120 g)	190°C	16 to 20	Meatballs (7-cm)	190°C	10
Filet Mignon (250 g)	200°C	18-20	Ribeye, bone in (2-cm, 250 g)	200°C	12 to 15
Flank Steak (700 g)	200°C	13	Sirloin steaks (2-cm, 350 g)	200°C	10 to 14
London Broil (900 g)	200°C	20 to 28	Beef Eye Round Roast (1.8 kg)	200°C	45 to 55
Meatballs (2-cm)	190°C	7			

Pork and Lamb

Item	Temp (°C)	Time (mins)	Item	Temp (°C)	Time (mins)
Loin (900 g)	180°C	55	Bacon (thick cut)	200°C	6 to 10
Pork Chops, bone in (2-cm, 200 g)	200°C	13	Sausages	190°C	15
Tenderloin (450 g)	190°C	15	Lamb Loin Chops (2-cm thick)	200°C	8 to 12
Bacon (regular)	200°C	5 to 7	Rack of lamb (600-1000 g)	190°C	23

Fish and Seafood

Item	Temp (°C)	Time (mins)	Item	Temp (°C)	Time (mins)
Calamari (250 g)	200°C	5	Tuna steak	200°C	7 to 10
Fish Fillet (2-cm, 250 g)	200°C	12	Scallops	200°C	5 to 7
Salmon, fillet (200 g)	190°C	12-14	Prawn	200°C	5
Swordfish steak	200°C	10			

Frozen Foods

Item	Temp (°C)	Time (mins)	Item	Temp (°C)	Time (mins)
Onion Rings (350 g)	200°C	9	Fish Fingers (300 g)	200°C	11
Thin Chips (550 g)	200°C	13	Fish Fillets (1-cm, 300 g)	200°C	15
Thick Chips (500 g)	200°C	20	Chicken Nuggets (350 g)	200°C	10
Mozzarella Sticks (300 g)	200°C	8	Breaded Prawn	200°C	9
Pot Stickers (300 g)	200°C	8			

Appendix 3: Recipes Index

A

apple
Modern Ploughman's Lunch / 15
Cider-Braised Veggie Sausage Hotpot / 34
Apple Hazelnut Galette / 45
Apple Crumble Cupcakes / 49
asparagus
Asparagus and Parma Ham Spirals / 19
Toasted Sourdough and Hazelnut Asparagus / 29
aubergine
Veggie Moussaka / 33
avocado
Luxurious Baked Avocado Eggs / 10

B

bacon
Sizzling Bacon and Egg Muffins / 9
Crispy Grilled Bacon Sandwiches / 10
Crispy Cheese and Bacon Scones / 12
baked bean
Savoury Baked Beans on Cheesy Toast / 13
banana
Banana Hot Cross Bread / 63
beef brisket
Ale-Braised Beef Brisket / 22
beef short rib
Whisky Glazed Short Ribs / 26
beetroot
Beetroot and Lentil Veggie Burgers / 33
Bengali Beetroot Croquettes / 40
black pudding
Crispy Black Pudding Bites / 9
blackberry
Blackberry Millefeuille Delight / 48
blueberry
Blueberry Bliss Cheesecake / 44
Brussels sprouts
Creamy Bacon Sprouts / 53
button mushroom
Creamy Boursin-Stuffed Mushrooms / 37

C

carrot
Savoury Nut Carrot Bites / 34
cauliflower
Golden Honey-Tahini Cauliflower / 30
Satay-Style Whole Cauliflower / 32
Spiced Cauliflower Fritters / 41
cherry
Black Forest Bakewell Delight / 45
cherry tomato
British Breakfast Frittata / 8
chestnut mushroom
Grilled Herb Mushrooms on Toast / 12
chicken breast
Thai Coconut Chilli Chicken / 23
Satay Roast Chicken / 28
Chicken and Mushroom Mini Pies / 57
Garlic Butter Chicken Kiev / 60
chicken thigh
Lemon Zest Herb Chicken / 16
chuck steak
Pub-Style Beef and Ale Hand Pies / 20
clementine
Halloumi Clementine Salad / 54
courgette
Courgette and Ricotta Melts / 15
Crispy Veggie Galette / 17
Summer Vegetable Gratin / 35
crab
Crab Croquettes with Romesco Sauce / 55
currant
Festive Fruit Cake / 56

D, F-H, K

dark chocolate
Chocolate Yule Log / 50
fig
Honeyed Figs with Sesame Crunch / 48
gammon steak
Grilled Gammon with Garden Peas and Silky Hollandaise / 22
guinea fowl
Parsnip and White Wine Guinea Fowl / 25
ham
Deluxe Ham and Cheese Toastie / 17
kipper
Smoky Kippers and Eggs / 18

L

lamb
Quick Shepherd's Pie / 18
lamb chop
Minty Air Fried Lamb Chops / 21

lamb shoulder
Lamb Shoulder Feast with Peppered Rosemary Jus / 25
leek
Creamy Baked Leeks / 56
lemon
Lemon Meringue Tartlets / 43
Zesty Lemon Drizzle Cake / 47
Classic Lemon Tart / 49
Lemon Curd Cake / 59

M-O

mushroom
Herbed Polenta and Mushroom Bake / 35
nut
Spicy Nut and Seed Mix / 39
onion
Cheesy Onion Pie / 21

P

parsnip
Marmite and Poppy Seed Parsnips / 29
pear
Pear and Chestnut Festive Stuffing / 30
Pear and Butter Puff Strudel / 44
pepper
Colourful Stuffed Pepper Medley / 27
Paneer and Pepper Skewers with Gooseberry Raita / 42
pork belly
Barbecue Pork Belly / 24
pork loin roast
Orchard Roast Pork with Cider Apples / 28
pork sausage
Sausage and Bean Breakfast Casserole / 11
potato
Orchard Pork Sausages with Rustic Mash / 19
Spiced Aloo Tikki Bites / 31
Smoky Chilli Chips with Garlic Dip / 37
Crispy Pakora Bites / 38
Chaat Platter / 42
Lemon Sage Potatoes Anna / 55

R

rhubarb
Rhubarb and Custard Brioche Bake / 43

S

salmon
Dill and Lemon Infused Salmon / 27
sausage
Full English Breakfast Traybake / 11
Sumptuous Sausage and Egg Casserole / 14
Golden Air-Fried Scotch Eggs / 36
Favourite Sausage Roll Wreath / 57
Savoury Sausage Rolls / 61
sea bream
Herb-Crusted Sea Bream / 24
sirloin steak
Peppered Steak and Radish Salad / 58
smoked mackerel
Smoked Mackerel Melts / 58
smoked salmon
Smoked Salmon Crostini / 40
Cheesy Salmon Wreath / 52
Salmon Terrine Delight / 63
spinach
Baked Spinach and Feta Omelette / 13
strawberry
Eton Mess Roll / 59
swede
Hasselback Swede Gratin / 51

T

tofu
Balsamic Glazed Tofu and Gnocchi / 32
tomato
Grilled Cheese and Tomato Breakfast Sandwiches / 14
topside of beef
Herb-Crusted Roast Beef / 62
turkey
Turkey Koftas with Cranberry Dip / 52
turkey breast
Bacon-Wrapped Roast Turkey / 50

V

venison
Game Terrine with Brandy Prunes / 53

W

walnut
Walnut Cheese Rolls / 54
white chocolate
Caramelised White Chocolate Dream Cake / 46
white fish
Herb-Crusted Air-Fried Fish / 16
whitebait
Five-Spice Whitebait / 38
whole chicken
Lemon-Thyme Roasted Chicken / 26
Lemon Herb Roast Chicken / 62
whole duck
Duck with Orange Sauce / 23

Printed in Great Britain
by Amazon